MOTORCYCLE JOURNEYS THROUGH
NEW ENGLAND

You Don't Have to Get Lost to Find the Good Roads

Second Edition

by Martin C. Berke

A Whirlaway Book
Whitehorse Press
North Conway, New Hampshire

Interior photography by the author unless
otherwise noted.

A Whirlaway Book. Second edition published
February 1994 by
　Whitehorse Press
　P.O. Box 60
　North Conway, New Hampshire 03860 U.S.A.
　Phone: 603-356-6556 or 800-531-1133
　FAX: 603-356-6590

Whirlaway and Whitehorse Press are trademarks
of Kennedy Associates.

ISBN   0-9621834-8-2

5 4 3 2

Printed in the United States of America

Dedication

I would like to dedicate this book to Pauline. Tara, who has

the ability to keep me young while aging me. And Sonia.

Acknowledgements

I want to thank the many people who helped me make my inspiration into a book: Dan Kennedy, my publisher, for the opportunity. Fawn Fitter, my editor, for helping me make it a better book. The open, honest people I met on the road who shared with me the feel, not just the facts, of their home towns. And finally, to the NightCAP (Children At Play), our gang.

Contents

Introduction

This book is for and about motorcycle journeys. It creates destinations and helps you maximize your enjoyment while touring New England by motorcycle, whether you've been touring for years or are just starting to dabble from the seat of a crotch rocket.

A journey, unlike a trip, is an opportunity for wandering and exploring new territory with all five senses. The intent of this book is to get you going, to present choices, and to encourage you to venture on your own.

I do not list every bump in the road, or even every great motorcycling road. This book, however, is written with the special needs of motorcyclists in mind: you'll find comments on the quality of roads, service facilities, breakfast places, and other important matters. As for the routes, think of them as a starting point, giving you the benefit of my experiences while allowing you to build your own repertoire of favorite journeys. Depending on how much time you have available, the kind of terrain you prefer, and of course, your whim, you will quickly build your own custom journeys.

New England is a region of contrast and diversity. The compactness of New England allows you to venture from 6000-foot mountain peaks to beaches on the Atlantic Ocean, and from Yankee seaports to the largest body of fresh water outside the Great Lakes, on the same day!

The variety of terrain—lakes, rivers, islands, ocean, and mountains—provides a rich backdrop for touring adventures. The mountains give us roads with tight ascending and descending curves. In the valleys you can meander through rolling farmlands that seem to go on without end, where you can't tell what's over the other side until you're there. Little-used river and lake roads hug the water's edge so tight you'd think you were riding a snake's back. Honky-tonk seaside towns sit beside the original "perpetual wave machine."

There are two general rules for choosing roads in New England. The first is that north-south routes follow rivers on valley floors. These roads will vary from sharp curves to smooth lazy turns, but they tend to be flat, while east-west roads are characterized by mountain ascents and descents, tighter curves, switchbacks, and rougher roads. The second rule: route numbers with the greater number of digits and/or with letters further down the alphabet tend to be smaller and have tighter curves. For example, Route 402 or 17F will be more fun than Route 42 or 17A!

Organization of the Book

The book contains two kinds of information: descriptions of the journeys themselves, and useful or important "on the road" information. The journeys described in this book take advantage of the compactness of New England, the variety of its terrain, and its extensive road system.

The roads in New England, like those in most older settlements of the world, tend to follow what existed before the advent of the internal combustion engine. Most of the little rural roads are paved cow paths. Although this school of road design can be a source of frustration in a city environment (as anybody will understand on a first attempt to navigate the city of Boston), in a rural setting we are grateful that cows don't walk a straight line.

Each "journey" described in this book includes three to five day-long "loops." At the beginning of each journey, an orientation section gives you a look at the geography and/or history of the particular region, something to provide a little context to the ride.

I have designed the journeys to be flexible. My objective is to expose you to New England's entire geographical menu. If you have a week or two, sip and savor the full five-loop banquet. Got a weekend? Try a couple of loops from the *à la carte* menu. Sneaking off for a day trip? Taste some of the highlights to go.

As a matter of safety, comfort, and personal preference, I like to establish a base camp so I can travel more nimbly during the day without my touring gear, and give myself more time to ride by not having to set up or break down my gear each day. I camp as much as possible because the experience immerses me in the environment. For each journey, the loops bring you back to a chosen home base. I have identified my base camps for each journey; however, there are no rules here! You can start and finish anywhere you choose. There are plenty of places to stay on the journeys. Depending on your budget and personal preferences, your choices range from campgrounds, to motels, to B & B's, to inns. Have fun exploring!

With a few longer exceptions, each loop within a particular journey equals a day's ride. I tried to design a full day of riding for each loop, including unique places, attractions, or points of interest, and bring you back to home base.

The loops themselves average between 150 and 200 miles and will have tight twisties, open road, scenic vistas, and a place or two to stop and exercise all five senses. If your style leans toward marathon riding, try combining a couple of loops. If your style is to point to and appreciate every tree, rock, and man-made structure in the universe, you can abbreviate the loops.

I have included for each loop the directions; a loop drawing; a description of the ride; information on obtaining the best state maps; places to stay; places of interest; and finally, useful road information such as motorcycle dealerships, emergency numbers, and medical facilities (I know its a bummer to think about, but . . .).

I have organized this book so it's easy to use even while you're riding. The book fits into the map case of your tank bag. The sketches of the journeys are roughly to scale; however, a good road map is indispensable for finding your own special squiggly, not to mention the way home.

Dollars and Sense

I chose the loops and the places to stay, stop, or eat within the journeys based on the following criteria:

Safety. This consists of road surface, amount of four-wheel traffic, and/or remoteness. Special safety factors for a specific journey, if there are any (for example, moose in the Notches Journey), are in the orientation section for the specific journey.

Comfort. This includes physical accommodations, natural beauty and charm, and social acceptance of motorcyclists. If the place is in this book, I was well received.

Value. Assuming that most of us seek the biggest bang for our touring buck, quality of service and cost were criteria in choosing accommodations, food, and attractions. Where restaurants are mentioned, one "$" is cheap, two are moderate, three are expensive.

I am always interested in your opinions. If you have favorite roads to suggest, ideas to make this book better, or other helpful hints to offer, please send them along to me, care of the publisher. Thanks, and keep the rubber side down!

Marty

Goin' Downeast

Maine, the largest of the six New England states, has a total area about the size of the other five states combined. One county, Aroostook, is larger than Connecticut and Rhode Island together. This journey will easily take five days, not including travel to and from Mt. Desert Island, our home base.

The state is 320 miles long, but exploring the harbors, coves, points, and peninsulas of the shoreline (3,478 miles) is the equivalent of driving cross-country. Because of the forces of moon, sun, tides, weather, and their interaction with this vast shoreline, a number of natural attractions are a question of timing. For example, East Quoddy Head Light on Campobello Island can only be reached during the 1½ hours on either side of slack tide. You can pick up tidal charts at most local tourist centers. I will highlight the cosmic timing, along with the attraction it affects, in the loop descriptions. Slack tide is dead low tide and flood tide is high tide.

Maine is the largest blueberry-growing state in the nation (don't worry, blueberry pancakes are discussed in the individual loops). It is nationally famed for its lobsters; over 28 million pounds of lobsters were harvested in 1990. The total Maine catch of clams, quohogs, lobster, and fin fish was approximately 1.7 billion pounds for 1990. Get ready for some good downeast riding and down home eating!

Before you take off, you should have these tidbits of information. First, Maine drivers have a peculiar habit of using at least two-thirds of the available road surface to get from one place to another. You often see signs warning KEEP TO RIGHT. Please do so, because

Maine drivers don't! Anticipate and take the inside line on all curves.

Second: downeast Maine has its own language. The following dictionary of terms will help you understand directions, make conversation, and prevent you from saying "huh?" a million times. Thanks to "Bob the Lobster" at Ruth & Wimpy's Kitchen for his patience in teaching a fromaway (a foreigner, not from the state of Maine).

ayah – Means yes, most of the time. It does not necessarily mean agreement.

apiece – A mile; a further; a measurement. For example, "Down the rud apiece."

rud – Highway, byway.

cah – Something to contain lobsters being held for market; an auto.

by thunder – An expletive; cuss word.

butt-sprung – Condition of aged male whose rear end drags.

mite – Much or many.

lowry – Overcast weather; sour-puss.

crittah – Any animal, including Democrats.

in full sail – A well-endowed female.

tunk – To hit. For example, "Tunk it a mite."

cripes – Candy-coated cuss word.

summah – Between spring and fall.

messo – Unit o' measurement. For example, "Messo clams."

gaud – Cuss word, mostly directed at elected officials.

boondocks – Land more than 500 yards from the shore or south of Kittery.

ablow – Wind. For example, "Look out, its going to be a whopper of ablow."

reach – Long body o' water between hunks of land; what you do when the blueberry pancakes are apt to get by you.

pound – Place where lobsters are stored; a unit o' measurement.

crik – Small stream; pain in the neck.

spleeny – Milk-toast type; coward; applied mostly to husbands.

Ruth & Wimpy's Kitchen, Route 1, Sullivan, Maine

yad – Land in front of or around house.

cussed – Term of endearment used to describe New Yorkers, Vermonters and crittahs from Massachusetts.

cottage – Summer person's mansion.

camp – Maine person's cottage.

shuck – To divest clams of their innards. You shuck clams to make chowdah!

flats – Land offshore, fragrant at low tide.

The third piece of important information is how and where to eat lobster. The only type of establishment that counts when you eat Maine lobster is a lobster pound. You will recognize a lobster pound by the billowing smokestacks and steam rising from large washbasins of boiling sea water. As you enter the wooden shack, you are immediately enveloped by the aroma of chowdah, buttah, steamahs (clams) and, of course, lobstahs. The sharp cracks coming from the long wooden family-style tables tweak your interest about what's going on o' yondah. As you approach the "order here" counter, you watch the small net bags of red lobsters returning from their fate, being grabbed by . . . NUMBER FOUR! The menu is *à la carte*, written on the blackboard. You buy your soft drinks, corn, butter, and bread individually. To save money, I bring all the fixings and cold drinks. It is done all the time by the experienced lobster warrior.

When it's your turn, address the cooler or salt-water trough with your index finger poised, and begin the hunt for your Maine course. Focus, aim, aannd . . . point. You order and buy the lobster by the pound (make sure it's hard shell because they molt). Two pounds is a good meal, three is gluttonous, four is a massacre (and a tougher tasting bird).

The wait person will net and bag your choice, give you a number, carry your catch to the salt-water vats you passed on the way in, and drop them in. You'll get a call in about 12 to 15 minutes. You will receive your lobster in a baking pan similar to a corn bread pan. This is your dinner plate. Tear off the claws, grab your nutcracker and join the cacophony of the dining room. There is meat in the claws, in the knuckles attached to the claws, in the small eight legs, inside the body at the junction of the small legs and body (don't eat the gray fibrous pieces, they're the lungs), and in the tail. Don't forget the five little fan tails. It is a messy, sensual experience, and everybody gets into it. There is usually a communal sink in the dining room to hose yourself down. *Bon Appetit!*

Our home base for the Downeast Journey is the **Mt. Desert Campground** on Mt. Desert Island. Note: Although the name of this popular area is spelled like an arid place, it is pronounced like the diet-buster. Nestled at the top of **Somes Sound,** most sites have platforms, many sitting high above or directly on the water. The scent of the ocean and the cry of a gull reflect the journey's theme.

East Quoddy Head Light

Frenchman Bay

The Sunrise County Loop

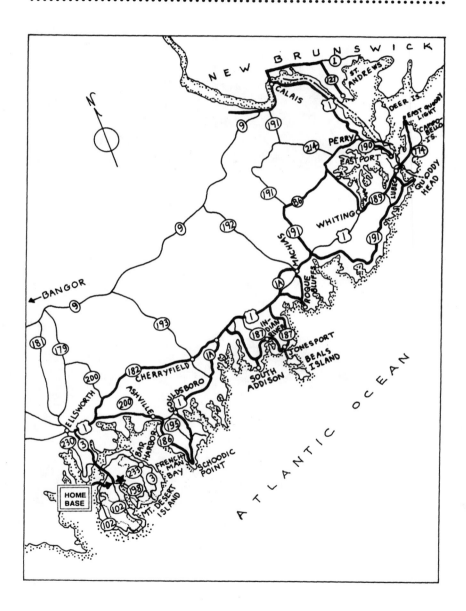

The Sunrise County Loop

· ·

Distance   *310 miles (517 kilometers)*

Speed   *10 to 65* MPH *(17 to 108* KPH*)*

Highlights   *Sweeping ocean views, small back roads through pine forests, small village and harbor atmosphere*

The Route from Mt. Desert Campground

→ Route 198 north to Route 102/198 north at Somesville, Me.

→ Route 102/198 north to Route 3 west at junction.

→ Route 3 west to Route 1 north at Ellsworth.

→ Route 1 north to Route 186 south at Ashville.

→ Route 186 north to Route 1 north at Gouldsboro.

→ Route 1 north to Route 1A north at Milbridge.

→ Route 1A north to Route 1 north at Harrington.

→ Route 1 north to Addison Road at Columbia.

→ Keep right and follow signs to South Addison on access road (no name).

→ Turn around and return from South Addison.

→ At intersection of South Addison access road bear right onto Addison Road. You will be heading northeast to the village of Indian River.

→ Route 187 south at Indian River.

→ At T in West Jonesport take a left (no sign for 187 continuation). * (See Route Detour 1)

→ Route 187 north to Route 1 north at junction.

→ Route 1 north to ROQUE BLUFFS STATE PARK sign.

→ At T go right; follow signs to Roque Bluffs State Park.

→ Return to same access road.

→ Bear right at fork (sign for MACHIAS) to Route 1 north.

→ Route 1 north to Route 191 east at East Machias.

→ Bear right at South Trescott (follow coast) where Route 191 bears left.

→ Take right over causeway (almost a 180 degree turn) to Quoddy Head Road and Quoddy Head State Park.

→ Return via Quoddy Head Road to intersection.

→ Bear right at intersection of Quoddy Head Road. Follow signs to Route 189 east and Lubec

→ Route 189 east to Canadian border at Campobello Island, New Brunswick.

→ Canadian Route 774 east, bear right at T. Follow signs for WILSON'S BEACH and HEAD HARBOR to East Quoddy Head.

→ Return via Route 774 west.

→ Route 774 west to Route 189 west at U.S. border.

→ Route 189 west to Route 1 north at Whiting, Me.

→ Route 1 north to Route 190 east at Perry.

→ Route 190 east to Eastport.

→ Return Route 190 west.

→ Route 190 west to Route 1 south. ** (See Detour 2)

→ Route 1 south to Route 86 west at junction.

→ Route 86 west to Route 191 east (it's a left) at junction.

→ Route 191 south to Route 1 south at East Machias.

→ Route 1 south to Route 1A south at Machias.

→ Route 1A south to Route 1 south at junction.

→ Route 1 south to Route 182 west at Cherryfield.

→ Route 182 west to Route 1 south at intersection.

→ Route 1 south to Route 3 east at Ellsworth.

→ Route 3 east to Route 198/102 south at junction.

→ Route 198/102 to Route 198 south and home.

* Route Detour 1

→ Take Right to Beals Island at Beals Island Bridge.

→ Take left at end of bridge on coastal road. Go to Kelly's Point and return to bridge via same coastal road.

→ Cross Beals Island and rejoin Route 187 north.

** Route Detour 2

→ Route 1 north to Calais, Maine.

→ Cross Canadian border, rejoining Route 1 north at Saint Stephen, New Brunswick.

→ Route 1 north to Route 127 south at junction.

→ Route 127 south to Saint Andrews, (by-the-sea).

→ Return to Saint Stephen and Calais, Maine via Route 1 south.

The Sunrise County Loop is at least a two-day trip. Even that amount of time doesn't give you enough opportunity to absorb the grandeur and subtle beauty of the easternmost section of the United States, with its projection into the North Atlantic. Pick a few spots and spend the time.

On my first night at the campground, I fell asleep to the sound of a comforting and enveloping foghorn, not realizing what it portended for the morning: fog. Fog is common in Maine, but you can keep it from restricting your travel by starting your trip inland. This loop can be done in reverse order so you reach the best scenery later in the day, after the fog has burnt off.

As you leave Mt. Desert Island via Route 3 over the Thompson Island Bridge and flats (see definition of flats), funky gift shops and touristy motels line the road. Among this tourist litter are a string of lobster pounds. The best for value with the largest selection is **Trenton Bridge Lobster Pound,** just over the bridge on the mainland. Lunch or dinner, the blackboard menu reads lobster.

Route 1 north provides glimpses of Frenchman Bay and, on a clear day, the silhouette of the mountains on Mt. Desert Island. Route 186, freshly paved, leads you down **Schoodic Peninsula** to **Winter Harbor** and the easternmost portion of **Acadia National Park.** The primeval spruce forest abuts the shoreline, where unstoppable ocean waves crash endlessly against the immovable granite coast. Just after a storm and/or in conjunction with a full moon, the tide is particularly dramatic (bring your rain gear, as the ocean spray makes you feel like you have the forward watch on the prow). The 6½-mile road is one-way around Schoodic Point. It's worth a full roll of film. Acadia National Park shares the peninsula with a large naval communications facility.

Rejoin Route 186 (don't bother with the Route 195 to Corea impulse) and grab Route 1 north to continue your game of hide and seek with the coast. Route 1A,

Trenton Bridge Lobster Pound is the best!

less traveled than Route 1, cuts through the salt marshes of Narraguagus and Pleasant Bays to Harrington. Just after Harrington on Route 1 is **Perry's Seafood,** a good place for your basic two-egg breakfast special.

Two miles up Route 1 from Perry's is a blinking light with a small sign on the right pointing the way to Addison and South Addison. This little mini-loop brings you in and around quaint little coves with nothing but lobster pot floats to indicate civilization is close at hand. In South Addison, if you are inclined to do some home cooking, go to end of the dock in Eastern Harbor and buy fresh lobster right off the boat.

Jonesport is a picturesque harbor best appreciated from the Beals Island side. The old wharves in Jonesport and on Beals Island are graying weathered structures piled high with lobster traps and markers. They look exactly like you imagine they would.

Back on Route 1 north, just after the town of Jonesboro, is the road marked by a sign to **Roque Bluffs State Park.** The Park is six miles off Route 1. It has one of the few sandy beaches on the rocky Maine coast. Just across the street from the salt-water beach, you can rinse in a fresh-water pond. That is, if you dare go for a brisk 55-degree average ocean temperature dip! It's a place to stretch your legs and get rid of "NumButt," although with the water that cold, you'll probably be numb again in no time.

Returning to Route 1 north, passing through the town of Machias, pick up any provisions you need. It is the last sizable town on the loop with reasonable prices for commodities such as batteries and film.

Route 191 south, starting east of Machias, is an exceptional road. Smooth and isolated, it hugs the craggy shoreline at a height that provides ocean vistas the entire way to West Quoddy Head. Those high towers off to the south just after North Cutler, which look like the superstructure to a football stadium, are an array of radio towers. This 2,800-acre U.S. Navy base provides communications to all units of the fleet in the North Atlantic, Arctic, and Europe. There are 26 major towers forming two arrays. Each center tower is 980 feet tall, just 40 feet shorter than the Empire State Building.

At South Trescott be sure to keep right as Route 191 veers inland. Just after the split, you come to Bailey's Mistake, a small coastal harbor. Captain Bailey, it seems, made the mistake (with considerable use of his sextant and compass one foggy night) of running aground

Schoodic Point

Fog at Machias

seven miles off course from the Lubec Narrows. The next morning, under clear skies, Captain Bailey could see he was in the center of a mile-wide bay and not in the Narrows between Lubec and Campobello Island. With his ego in worse shape than his ship, the captain and crew unloaded their timber cargo, built homes, and never returned to their home port of Boston.

Between South Trescott and **West Quoddy Head State Park,** two of the ten miles of the road is dirt. It's packed dirt roadbed and easy to negotiate, although the maps don't show it as unpaved.

The West Quoddy Head Lighthouse is the eastern-most point in the continental United States. This park is a must-see. The candy-striped lighthouse was built in 1858. The beacon, 83 feet above sea level, can be seen for twenty miles at sea. A constant reminder of danger, the groaner buoy, one mile offshore, sounds a continuous warning for Sail Rock.

Finback, Humpback and Northern Right whales migrate here each summer from their winter habitat off the northeastern coast of South America. The whales mate and calve in this part of the Bay of Fundy.

The lighthouse and pathways sit on top of 90-foot cliffs. The waves crash on outcrops both near and far, and seals play or sun themselves on these small oases. Bring binoculars if you have them to try to see the Canadian islands of Campobello and Grand Manan.

Lubec is the easternmost *town* in the United States, although Eastport, on the other side of Cobscook Bay, lays claim to the title of the easternmost *city* in the United States. Actually, the Aleutian Islands are the easternmost part of the U.S., since a part of them are across the international date line in the Pacific. You probably should not mention that small detail in either Eastport or Lubec.

Lubec's main claim to fame, though, is being the gateway to **Campobello Island,** the childhood summer home of Franklin Delano Roosevelt. It was here that he contracted polio and was carried off the island; he made only two visits afterward.

Cross over the FDR Memorial Bridge (you are leaving the United States) and you must stop for Canadian Immigration and Customs. Ditto on the return with the U.S. entry. The Canadian requirements for entry by U.S. citizens at this time is a picture I.D. The U.S. requirement for entry by Canadian citizens for visitor status is the same. If you are neither a U.S. nor a Canadian citizen, please call U.S. and Canadian Immigration departments for your requirements. If you are entering either country for any reason other than a visit, call ahead!

Stop at the information booth on the right just up the road apiece. The attendants have maps, tidal charts, and information on the island attractions, New Brunswick, and Canada. Exchange some money there; it's the best rate you'll get.

The two major attractions on Campobello Island are the **Roosevelt Campobello International Park** and the **East Quoddy Head Light.**

The free park has a 15-minute orientation film on the history of FDR and his relationship with Campobello Island. The "summer cottage" is refurbished in actual period pieces. The tour guides embellish the history with flair and enthusiasm. It is easy to imagine yourself playing and living in the cottage as a kid.

East Quoddy Head Light is seven miles past the Park at the end of the island (bear right at T). Keep going even after the pavement turns into a narrow dirt road. If you time it to arrive at slack tide (about 1¼ hours on either side of low tide), you can climb a series of metal ladders to get to the lighthouse. The views are sterling, with harbors on both sides of the point, lobster boats pulling up their traps, fishing boats returning from the sea with gulls whirling above in the wind. An excursion worth the dismount. A note of cosmic caution: the tide rises five feet an hour. If you get caught on the point, you'll have to wait eight or nine hours before you can return.

To return to the U.S., grab Route 189 out of Lubec and drive the 40 miles around Cobscook Bay to Eastport. Route 190 is a long causeway with lovely views of

FDR Memorial Bridge, connecting Canada and the U.S.

The Roosevelt summer cottage

spruce-dotted islands. The town of Eastport is a picturesque sea town. The main drag is Water Street, which runs parallel to the ocean, 20 feet from tides that range from 16 to 22 feet. One of the effects of these extreme tides is **Old Sow,** the second largest whirlpool in the world and one of the most dangerous. Created by tidal currents coming together between Eastport and Deer Island, New Brunswick, Old Sow has tipped over a tanker and swallowed many small ships. To see it, take a left on Water Street (as you face the ocean) out to the Bayview Cemetery, or off Clark Street. Old Sow is best seen about an hour and half before flood tide between Dog Island Point and Deer Island, N.B. Another good spot for observing tidal flows is Reversing Falls in West Pembroke.

Returning, head west on Route 190, then take Route 1 south and pick up Route 86 west, a small swath of asphalt cut through some very large pine stands. The curves come quickly and then the road straightens, then tight curves return, then it's back to wailing. Route 86 and Route 191 that follow are a typical example of the "Maine 1965 bomber with no shocks negotiating corners without heed to oncoming traffic" syndrome. Caveat Rider!

On Routes 191, 1, and 1A south of Machias, on the north side of the road, you'll notice a curious, low-brush, almost surreal moonscape. These are the famed blueberry barrens of Maine. In late summer, these rolling flatlands are a sea of blue. During late August, local and migrant workers (mostly the Micmac Indian tribe from New Brunswick) work from dawn to dusk to harvest the entire blueberry crop in three to four weeks. In mid- to late September the barrens ignite into flame red and scarlet, turning their majestic fall colors earlier than the rest of the surrounding foliage.

Route 182, a Maine scenic highway, fords streams, cuts across Tunk Lake, and offers the same untamed beauty inland as Maine offers on its shores. As Route 182 reenters civilization, the **Franklin Trading Post** appears. The blueberry pancakes, biscuits, and simple acceptance of a stranger made my $2.35 breakfast a real bargain. I asked for a receipt only to get smiles on both sides of the counter. It seems the Franklin Trading Post has achieved what the corporate world is only striving for: a paperless environment!

It is an easy jaunt home from here.

For a downhome, downeast breakfast

Bar Harbor-Acadia National Park Loop

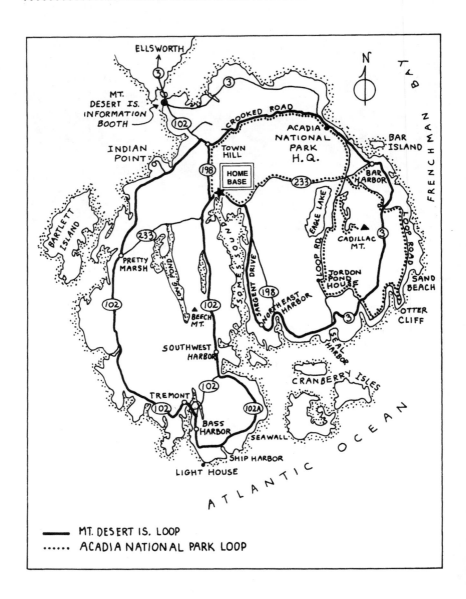

—— MT. DESERT IS. LOOP

...... ACADIA NATIONAL PARK LOOP

Bar Harbor–Acadia National Park Loop

Distance   *40 miles (64 kilometers)*

Speed   *5 to 25* MPH *(8 to 40* KPH)

Highlights   *Scenic ocean views, lakes, ponds, cliffs and mountains from sea level to highest point on the entire North American Atlantic coast*

The Route from Mt. Desert Campground

→ Route 198 north to right on Crooked Road at Town Hill.

→ Crooked Road to Route 3 east.

→ Route 3 east to Acadia National Park Visitor's Center at Hulls Cove.

→ Visitor Center's "spur" road to Loop Road.

→ Loop Road turns into Ocean Drive and back into Loop Road.

→ Loop Road to Cadillac Mountain Summit Road.

→ Return to Loop Road via the Summit Road descent.

→ Loop Road to signs for Bar Harbor exit at junction of Route 233 east.

→ Route 233 east to Bar Harbor.

→ Route 233 west to Route 198 north at junction.

→ Route 198 to home base.

Acadia National Park is the second most visited national park in the United States. Over four million people play in the park yearly. Do not be fooled by the mileage or speed of the Park Loop. The park beckons you to stop and explore with all your senses. It is a full day and night of geological splendor. A few suggestions: If you are going in July or August, do the loop before 10 a.m. or after 4 p.m., over a couple of days. The entry fee is $2.00 for a week!

The **Loop Road** is a two-lane, well paved road. About two-thirds of the loop is one-way. Parking is

Under the Loop Road, Acadia National Park

allowed in the right hand lane. Watch for people opening their driver's door without looking! You can and will want to stop every half-mile. I found the safest way to negotiate the traffic and pedestrians is to stay in the left-hand lane, put on my left blinker and let everybody deal with passing right, around me. This is a challenging loop to practice your slow drive racing skills. Take your time.

I found that wearing sneakers, although sacrificing a little protection, made the day's roam on foot easier than wearing my riding boots. Bring a picnic lunch; the

Tea time at Jordan Pond House

choices of where to dine in the outdoors are unparalleled and unlimited.

The loop begins at the visitor's center, where you can get a preview of the day's ride. The visitor's center has an excellent topographical model for orientation and sells a motorist's guide to the loop for 95 cents that provides a synopsis of the 13 most popular scenic spots and walking trails. The trails range from a pleasant 0.3 mile shore path along the 90-foot **Otter Cliffs** (I saw two pilot whales from the cliffs) to the iron rungs and ladders of the Precipice Trail. Be sure to read about the next stop before moving on; the guide contains information designed to alert you to features along the route, not just each stop on the route.

My two favorite spots are the **Jordan Pond House** and the **Cadillac Mountain Summit Road.** The Jordan Pond House is a civilized oasis in a wild and natural setting. The restaurant, which is two-thirds around the loop, serves tea and popovers on the back lawn every day from 2:30 to 5:00 p.m. The backdrop is the cliffs of Penobscot Mountain to the west, Bubble Mountain directly ahead to the north (a couple of miles up the road from Jordan Pond you can see Balanced Rock teetering on the ledge of Bubble Mountain), and Pemetic Moun-

Bar Harbor, from Cadillac Mountain

tain on the east. In the valley between is Jordan Pond, which laps the lawn by your table.

Cadillac Mountain is named for Antonine de la Mothe Cadillac, the Frenchman who took possession of this island in the late 1600s under a grant from Louis XIV. Later he founded Detroit, inspiring the name of the prestigious automobile. Cadillac Mountain, its summit, and the road to get you there will become very familiar to you, as you will climb the mountain many times. The climb, besides being a fun road with many switchbacks and cliff hangers, is one of the best ways to greet the sunrise and sunset. From Cadillac Mountain—at 1,530 feet, the highest point on the Atlantic Ocean north of Rio de Janeiro—you can be one of the first people in the United States to see a spectacular sunrise. And the next time you climb the mountain, you can see a magnificent sunset over the western part of the island. The barren granite summit, open until midnight with very little traffic after sunset, offers a surreal moonscape with vistas of Bar Harbor and the Atlantic.

If your astronomical timing is right, exactly two miles up the mountain, from the entrance to Summit Road, on the left, is a lookout where I saw an orange-crimson sunset to the west and a full moon rising in the east. I didn't know whether to howl or meditate! When I returned to the summit around 11:00 p.m., the wind was rising to 35 or 40 MPH. The two other people on the summit were chilled by the wind and sea air and left as soon as they arrived. As I was dressed for a 60 MPH wind chill factor anyway, I stayed to enjoy seeing my moon shadow dancing to the cosmic rhythms.

HINT: When the summit is crowded, go just behind the tourist shop to a trail head. Cross over the trail to the outcrop of rocks and you will discover two things: the crowds are about 300 yards away in the tourist-designated summit area, and you are about five feet higher. Just in front of the radio towers, on the outcrop where you are standing, is a rock formation that looks placed. It is the U.S Geological Marker for the summit!

Use Bar Harbor as a way station to and from your Cadillac Mountain jaunts. Bar Harbor is the commercial hub of the island, with many places to eat. **Jordan's,**

Jordan's Restaurant, Bar Harbor

on Cottage Street, is a good place for blueberry pancakes. In the evening, many establishments have live entertainment.

Gedy's, on Main Street down by the harbor, has an outdoor backyard game room. Inside, near the front, soloist singers entertain after 8:00 p.m.

The **Casino,** on Main Street by the park, offers headbanger music on weekends and a singer/guitarist on weekday nights.

The **Lompoc Cafe,** off Cottage Street, offers folk/mountain music. In the building next door, the cafe makes Bar Harbor Real Ale in its microbrewery. Tours are offered. The beer is very good, so plan to stay in one of the many inns or motels within walking distance if you decide to try it! The food is excellent, with a spicy hummus worth trying. The espresso and dessert bar make this a favorite late-night spot.

The **Unusual Cabaret** is just that. They offer fresh pastas each day with a serving of talented waiters and waitresses putting on musical plays after dinner.

And, if you really want to be BAD, the **Chocolate Emporium,** on Main Street opposite Cottage Street, is unbelievable. The aroma, display and the actual creation of the delights on the premises prohibit you from leaving without gorging yourself on the light chocolate, dark chocolate, and everything in between. Consider yourself forewarned!

The Casino,
Bar Harbor

The Mount Desert Island Western Loop

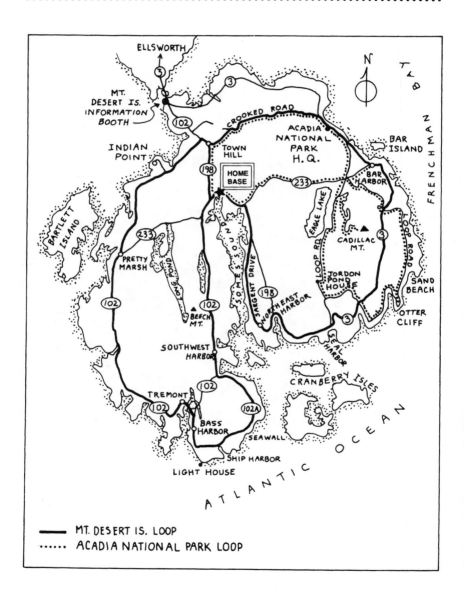

The Mount Desert Island Western Loop

Distance *60 to 70 miles (100 to 117 kilometers)*

Speed *5 to 55* MPH *(8 to 92* KPH*)*

Highlights *Open ocean, sea wall and coastal riding. Harbors, mountains and lake vistas.*

The Route from Mt. Desert Campground

➔ Route 198 north to Route 102/198 north at junction.

➔ Route 102/198 north to first left after Town Hill (see sign to Indian Point).

➔ Bear right at fork, heading south to Pretty Marsh.

➔ Rejoin Route 102 south at junction.

➔ Route 102 south to Route 102A east (it goes south) at junction.

➔ Route 102A east (now it goes north) to Route 102 north at junction.

➔ Route 102 north to Route 198 south at junction.

➔ Route 198 south to right on Sargent Drive.

➔ Sargent Drive to Harbor Drive at Northeast Harbor.

➔ Harbor Drive to Route 3 east (see signs for Route 3/Seal Harbor).

➔ Route 3 east to left on Crooked Road at junction.

➔ Crooked Road to Route 102/198 south at junction.

➔ Route 102/198 south to Route 198 south and home base.

The western side of Mount Desert Island has more quiet harbors and year-round residents and fewer commercial developments and tourists. It is just this lack of attention that appeals after battling the old tourist shuffle. The road to Pretty Marsh, a local favorite, runs through the pine forest on the way to the lowlands in the west. Pretty Marsh Harbor is a very small boat launch and not much else.

Bernard across
from Bass Harbor

Just after rejoining Route 102, you'll come to the Pretty Marsh picnic area, a serene, wooded spot on the ocean. In fact, all of Route 102 down to Bass Harbor is empty of anything retail. All the roads on the east side of Route 102 are either dirt or turn to dirt soon after you get on them. Route 102 itself has sweeping curves with a couple of hard turns and no interruptions all the way to Bass Harbor.

The **Seafood Ketch** has the best blueberry pancakes on the island. The batter is fluffy, loaded with berries, and cooked to perfection. With a front door moniker of "What food these morsels be," you gotta be good. The Seafood Ketch sits right on the harbor, but they don't allow fishing from the dining room windows.

The Bass Harbor Lighthouse is anti-climactic compared to others but is easy to get in and out to see.

Staying on Route 102A brings us to my favorite spot on this loop. The **Ship Harbor Nature Trail** is a 1.6-mile nature trail that opens up on the sea. The point faces south for sunning and the pink granite rocks are flat. The rocks where you sit seem to be contoured to your body. It's a good spot to nap, especially after breakfast and a stroll, with the sun warming your bones. The loop is short enough that you can take time for these types of digressions. The tough part is getting up to explore all the tidal pools. Rocks that are underwater in any part of the tidal flow are very slippery!

Route 102A continues past the **Seawall Campground,** one of two federal campgrounds in Acadia National Park. The campground gets its name from the natural sea wall built up over time just up the road. The picnic area across from the campground is a good place to see this formation.

Just before the village of Southwest Harbor, on the southern shore, is Manset, a one-working-street complex of restaurants, the Hinkley shipyard, and marina. The Moorings Restaurant boasts a "billion-dollar view." The pier offers the same view for less money. Watch the ships in dry dock being pulled in and out of the water.

Southwest Harbor is home to shipbuilders and a Coast Guard station. Opposite the Coast Guard station is Beals Lobster Wharf, where you can eat a lobster roll right on the pier. Just off Main Street is the **Wendell Gilley Museum of Bird Carving.** The museum houses an impressive display of Gilley's creations along with those of other noted carvers.

Echo Lake, Acadia National Park

Route 102 out of Southwest Harbor passes **Echo Lake** (good for swimming) and heads straight into Somesville, the oldest village on the island. Built at the headwaters of Somes Sound, the village has a historical society and is home to the Acadia Repertory Theater. Rounding Somes Sound and heading south you pick up Sargent Drive, which parallels the Sound. You are looking at the only fjord in the continental United States. Trailers and campers are excluded from the road and turnouts make stopping easy.

As you head south on **Sargent Drive,** getting closer to Northeast Harbor, you can see mailboxes but no houses to go with them. Northeast Harbor is the wealthiest place on Mt. Desert Island. The police force drives Volvos! The harbor is the usual turnaround spot for people sailing up the Maine coast.

The **Colonel's Restaurant** on Main Street offers excellent food at reasonable prices. You have to walk down the alley between two buildings to get to the restaurant. I had the broiled haddock filet, a large piece of FRESH fish on a homemade roll. The storefront is the Colonel's bakery, with outstanding desserts. The hermit (a raisin gingerbread cookie) was huge, with a strong, almost hot flavor.

Sargent's Drive by
Somes Sound

Route 3 east takes you back to Bar Harbor through Acadia. The road has lots of sweeping turns and twists. It is the best sustained bike riding road on the island. Besides, how can you resist another ride to Cadillac Mountain and a road named Crooked?

The "other"
Colonel's
Restaurant

Blue Hill and East Penobscot Bay Loop

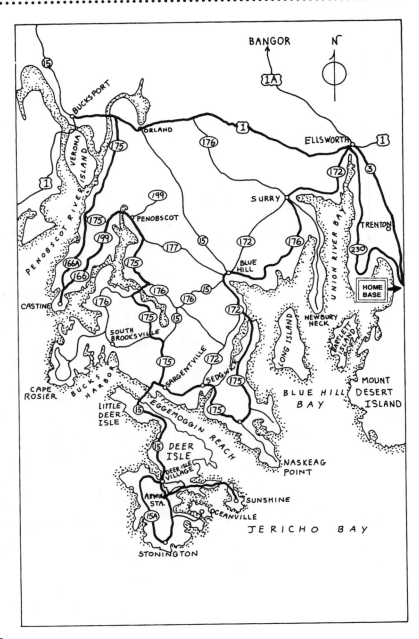

Blue Hill and East Penobscot Bay Loop

. . . .

Distance   *175 miles (292 kilometers)*

Speed   *5 to 65* MPH *(8 to 108* KPH*)*

Highlights   *Beautiful countryside, dramatic coastline, islands, and villages that range from bustling to bucolic*

The Route from Mt. Desert Campground

→ Route 198 north to Route 102/198 north at junction.

→ Route 102/198 north to Route 3 west at junction.

→ Route 3 west to Route 230 north after Trenton Bridge Lobster Pound.

→ Route 230 north to Route 1 south at Ellsworth.

→ Route 1 south to Route 172 south at Ellsworth.

→ Route 172 south to Route 176 west at Surry.

→ Route 176 west to Route 175/172 south at Blue Hill.

→ Route 175/172 south to Route 175 south at Blue Hill Falls.

→ Route 175 south (it looks north and west crossing the Benjamin River) to Route 15 south at Sargentville.

→ Route 15 south to Sunshine Road at Arwin Twin's Service Station.

→ Return via Sunshine Road to Route 15 south

→ Route 15 south to Stonington; at T take right onto Route 15A.

→ Bear left at fork, staying on West Main Street (Route 15A), the coastal road.

→ Rejoin Route 15A north at junction near Burnt Cove.

→ Route 15A north to Route 15 north at Deer Isle Village.

→ Route 15 north to Route 15/175 north at junction.

→ Route 15/175 north to Route 175 north at junction.

→ Route 175 north to Route 176 east/175 north at North Brooksville.

→ Route 176 east/175 north to Route 175 north at T (it's a left). Route 176 east is a right. Neither is marked at this time.

→ Route 175 north to Route 199 south above Penobscot.

➔ Route 199 south to Route 166 south. Follow signs to Castine.

➔ Route 166 north to Route 166A north at Castine.

➔ Route 166A north merges with Route 175 north.

➔ Route 175 north to Route 1 south at Orland.

➔ Route 1 south to Bucksport.

➔ Turn around.

➔ Route 1 north to Route 3 east at Ellsworth.

➔ Route 3 east to Route 102/198 south at junction.

➔ Route 102/198 south to Route 198 south and home base.

The Blue Hill Peninsula, Deer Isle, and East Penobscot Bay areas are the antithesis of the Mount Desert Island, Bar Harbor bustle. The distances are longer, rural and pristine. The largest town, off Route 1 on the loop, is Castine (and that's four streets by five streets).

Island hop across Eggemoggin Reach to Little Deer Isle, Deer Isle, Sunshine, and Mountainville over narrow causeways where the wind can whip up surf and sea spray as you fight cross currents. Other roads are smooth as silk gliding up, over, and down Union River, Blue Hill, and Penobscot Bays.

Bass Harbor

Morgan Bay

You leave Mount Desert Island by the now familiar Routes 198, 102, and 3. Then grab Route 230, up the road apiece from the Thompson Island Bridge (after the now famous Trenton Bridge Lobster Pound). Route 230 traces the east side of Union River Bay with glimpses of the shore. The road is rural, well conditioned, and avoids the more heavily traveled Route 3.

Entering Ellsworth (to be discussed later), take two quick lefts, the first at Route 1 and the second left at Route 172. You barely touch the town before slipping down the west side of the bay to the small village of Surry. Route 176 continues along the edge of the Blue Hill Peninsula through East Blue Hill to Blue Hill. Five routes intersect at various junctions within the town of Blue Hill. Don't get impatient; wait until you see the Route 175/172 south junction (the signs also read SOUTH BLUE HILL/BLUE HILL FALLS).

The Blue Hill Fair is more than 100 years old and is a major event in late August and early September. The fair inspired E. B. White's famous children's book, *Charlotte's Web.*

Farther south on Route 175 is the village of Brooklin and Naskeag Road. A small detour down the Naskeag Road brings you to a scenic point and harbor looping back to Route 175. The Brooklin General Store at the intersection of Route 175 and Naskeag Road has good coffee and company.

Route 175 wraps around the Benjamin River in Sedgwick, through Sargentville, and hooks inland at the intersection of Route 15. Take Route 15 south, crossing Eggemoggin Reach via a large suspension bridge, to the series of islands beginning with Little Deer Isle. This will add the unique experience of causeway driving to your road repertoire. These narrow roadways sitting on top of the ocean leave you totally at the mercy of the weather. The first time I crossed this set of causeways, "the breeze she be ablowin'," and the roads were wet with ocean spray, the waters lapping the edge of the roadway. The channels between the islands focus the wind across the causeways and the crosswinds created by the island formation are strong and unpredictable. The best way to judge the crosswinds is to watch the surface of the ocean as you approach the causeways.

Just after the town office in Deer Isle Village, and opposite the Arwin Twin's Service Station (it's a Gulf station, and Gulf seems to have a lock on the islands) is Sunshine Road. Sunshine Road brings you to Mountainville and Sunshine Island via a couple more causeways. Sunshine Road fans out at the end island to **Eaton's Pier** (sign on road), a lobster pound restaurant, in case you've worked up an appetite.

Returning to the center of Sunshine Road, follow signs to the **Haystack Mountain School of Crafts.** A visitor's center, open during the summer, displays work by artists and artisans who come from across the nation. Turn around and return via Sunshine Road to Route 15 south for Stonington. The largest village on the island, Stonington is still a working fishing harbor that depends on lobstering, scallop dragging, and boat building for its livelihood. There is a smattering of tourist stuff like galleries, inns, and restaurants. West Main Street splits off from Route 15A for a little coastal run before rejoining 15A at Burnt Cove. It returns to

Eaton's Pier Lobster Pound, Sunshine, Maine

Route 15 north at Deer Isle Village and takes you and your scooter back to the mainland.

Route 15 north to Route 175 north to Route 199 south rounds Northern Bay, pointing you into Castine. Signs for Castine begin appearing on Route 199.

Castine, an historic site on the National Register, is located at the mouth of the Penobscot River. Originally a trading post established by the Plymouth Pilgrims, it is the site of the worst U.S. Naval defeat in history. Trying to regain Castine from the British with a sea attack in 1779, the colonists lost 40 ships.

Maybe that's why the Maine Maritime Academy is located here. The **State of Maine** training vessel is open for half-hour tours when in port. In the harbor, small lobster boats bob next to vacationers' yachts and larger commercial ships.

Gilley's, on Water Street is the only year-round restaurant in Castine. Its clam chowder is rated a "best in class." The milk-based broth is light and instead of clams, Gilley's uses fresh shucked quohogs, a meatier shellfish, which to my taste are better than Maine clams. The cup was half full of quohogs, instead of just a few floating around in a sea of filler.

Routes 166A and 175 north give you views all along the coastline up to Route 1 in Orland. In Bucksport, just before the Waldo-Hancock suspension bridge where Route 1 crosses the Penobscot River, is the cemetery and headstone of Old Judge Buck. It seems that long ago, in the early 1700's, Buck sentenced a woman to be burned for witchcraft. Her curse at the burning was "so long my curse be upon thee and my sign upon thy tombstone." As the flames consumed her, a leg rolled out of the fire. As soon as Judge Buck's tombstone was set in place the leg appeared on it.

Route 1 north to Ellsworth is a straight shot at highway speed for 20 miles. If you can't make it back to the lobster pounds on Route 3 or you need a change of pace, there are two restaurants I recommend in Ellsworth. The first is **Maidee's International** on Main Street, a Chinese restaurant with live music ranging from folk to jazz, Wednesday through Saturday. The second is **Pop's Chowder House** in the mall just at the intersection of Routes 3 and 1. Although it lacks character, Pop's offers a fresh scallop, garlic, and clam pizza that is great. I hesitated too, but the combo and preparation will not disappoint you.

Gilley's, for great clam chowdah

Castine Harbor and the "State of Maine"

The curse on Judge Buck

Places of Interest

· ·

MAINE

Bar Harbor Jordan's Restaurant, 60 Cottage Street. Phone (207) 288-3586. Daily 6:30 a.m. to 2:00 p.m. Open May to October. Good food at good prices. The natives eat here. $$

Lompoc Cafe, 36 Rodick Street. Phone (207) 288-9392. Open daily 3:00 p.m. to 1:00 a.m. Open end of May to mid-October. Good desserts, coffee, and microbrewery. Entertainment at 9:00 p.m. $$

The Unusual Cabaret, 14½ Mt. Desert Street. Phone (207) 288-3306. Opens 6:00 p.m. with singing wait staff, shows starting at 9:00 p.m. Open from Mid-May to Mid-October. $8.00 for entrees, $6.00 for theater. $$

Bass Harbor Seafood Ketch Restaurant, on the harbor (follow signs off Route 102A). Phone (207) 244-7463. Daily 7:00 a.m. to 8:00 p.m. Open May through October. Best blueberry pancakes. $$

Castine Gilley's, Water Street. Phone (207) 326-4001. Daily 11:00 a.m. to 8:00 p.m.. Closed Tuesdays. Open year-round. Best Clam chowdah in town. $$

Deer Isle Eaton's Pier, Sunshine Road. Phone (207) 348-2489. Daily 11:00 a.m. to 7:00 p.m. Closed Sundays. Mid-May to October. $$

Ellsworth Maidee's International Restaurant, 156 Main Street. Phone (207) 667-6554. Daily 11:00 a.m. to midnight. Chinese food and entertainment. $$

Franklin Franklin Trading Post, Route 182. Phone (207) 565-3314. Daily 6:00 a.m. to 1:00 p.m.; Sunday 8:00 a.m. to 1:00 p.m. Open year-round. $

Mount Desert Island Acadia National Park, Visitor Center, Hulls Cove. Phone (207) 288-3338. The park is open year-round, the visitor center from May to October. $2.00 for a seven day pass. Mailing address for information is P.O. Box 117, Bar Harbor, 04609.

Jordan Pond House, Park Loop Road. Phone (207) 276-3316. Daily 11:30 a.m. to 9:00 p.m. Open May through October. Afternoon tea on the lawn. $$$

Mount Desert Campground, Route 198. Phone (207) 244-3710. Open from June to September. 175 sites, water view upon request, reservations recommended. $15.00–20.00.

Northeast Harbor The Colonel's Restaurant, Main Street. Phone (207) 276-5147. Daily 6:30 a.m. to 9:00 p.m. Open year-round. Fresh fish sandwiches and desserts. $$

Sullivan Ruth & Wimpy's Kitchen, Route 1. Phone (207) 422-3643. Open daily 11:00 a.m. to 10:00 p.m. Closing time varies. May to October. $$

Trenton Trenton Bridge Lobster Pound, Route 3, Trenton. Phone (207) 667-2977. Daily 10:00 a.m. to 9:00 p.m. Open May to Mid-October. The best lobster. $$

Travel Information

MAINE

Maine Publicity Bureau
Phone (800) 533-9595. Excellent state map, regional information by season, and booklets.

Maine State Ferry Service
Bass Harbor 04653. Phone (207) 596-2202 out of state; 800-521-3939 in state.

Maine State Parks
State House Station #22, Augusta 04333. Phone (207) 289-3824 for all state park information.Marine Atlantic Reservations Bureau

Bluenose Ferry to Nova Scotia, P.O. Box 250, North Sidney, Nova Scotia B2A 3M3. Ferry leaves from Route 3 in Bar Harbor. Written reservations only.

Emergency and Medical Assistance

....

MAINE

Bar Harbor Mt. Desert Island Hospital, Wayman Lane.
Phone (207) 288-5081.

Calais Calais Regional Hospital, Franklin Street.
Phone (207) 454-7521.

Eastport Eastport Health Care Center, Boynton Street. Phone (207) 853-6001.

Hulls Cove Acadia National Park Rangers, Route 3.
Phone (207) 288-3369, 288-3338, 288-3360.

Lubec Lubec Regional Medical Center, South Lubec Rd.
Phone (207) 733-5541; off-hours (207) 733-4321.

Machias Downeast Community Hospital, Upper Court Street. Phone (207) 255-3356.

Northeast Harbor Mt. Desert Island Police, Northeast Harbor Marina. Phone (207) 276-5111.

State Police in Orono Route 2. Emergency phone 800-432-7381; all other calls (207) 866-2122.

Cutting the White Mountain Notches

The White Mountains are located in the upper half of New Hampshire, bordering the Connecticut River and Vermont to the west and a small portion of Maine to the east. One third of New Hampshire is over 2,000 feet in elevation, and 84 percent, including the 1,100-square-mile White Mountain National Forest, is woods. The Appalachian Trail cuts through the range.

Here you will find some of the most dramatic mountain scenery in the Northeast. New Hampshire is the most mountainous of the New England states. In fact, Mount Washington is the highest peak in the Northeast (elevation 6,288 feet).

There are 12 notches in the White Mountains, 11 in New Hampshire and the twelfth, Grafton Notch, in Maine. A notch is a geological formation created thousands of years ago when a portion of the granite mountain range gave way under the pressure of glaciers. Breathtaking in their grandeur, dramatic to drive, the notches are blessed with a variety of good roads ranging from two-lane highways to narrow locals with more curves than a snake's back.

There are many places of all comfort levels to choose from in the region. The Conway area is quite crowded, due to the many outlet stores located there. While it's not my cup of tea, it provides an anchor for the Winnipesaukee Warmup Loop and the Western Notches Loop. I stayed south of Conway on Route 16 in

North Road, a
"long cut"

White Lake State Park, located in the White Mountain National Forest.

A vital safety tip: the moose population in northern New Hampshire and Maine is growing faster than the permits to trim it. Although the picture reads 170 collisions, that is deceiving, because I took the picture halfway through the 1991 season. To date, four motorcyclists have been killed. You will lose the war running into a moose. These animals can weigh up to a ton!

This ain't no
bull . . . winkle

Some advice shared by the locals: moose are nocturnal, so limit your night riding. If you must ride at night, lower your speed. Unlike deer, which freeze, moose put their heads down and bolt across the road, once they determine to go. Moose also tend to be long-legged; therefore, your headlight barely catches their belly hair. I was told to adjust my headlight just a hair higher, no pun intended, to catch their bodies.

The best way to spot moose is to scan the road side to side continuously, because they do blend into the surroundings. I asked about one of those high pitched, only-the-animals-hear whistles that attach to the frame. I was told they work, but fill up with bugs too fast to be relied upon. Forewarned is forearmed!

The Winnipesaukee Warmup Loop

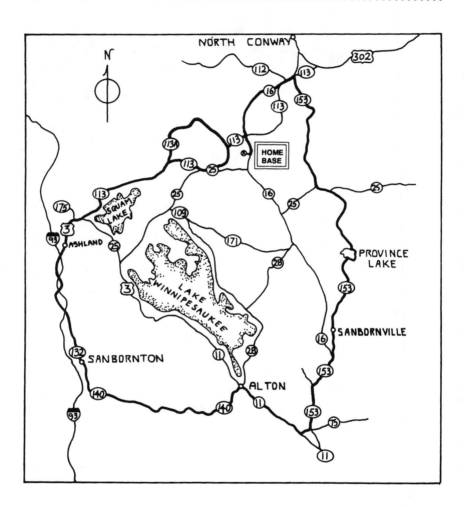

The Winnipesaukee Warmup Loop

Distance *150 miles (250 kilometers)*
Speed *20 to 60 MPH (33 to 100 KPH)*
Highlights *Curves, well paved, small hills*

The Route from White Lake State Park

→ Route 16 north to Route 153 south at Conway, N.H.
→ Route 153 south to Route 75 west at Farmington.
→ Route 75 west to Route 11 west.
→ Route 11 west to Route 140 west at Alton.
→ Route 140 west to Route 132 north at Sanbornton.
→ Route 132 north to Route 3 south at Ashland.
→ Route 3 south to Route 113 east at Holderness.
→ Route 113 east to Route 16 south at Chocorua. *
→ Route 16 south to White Lake State Park.

* Alternate route:

→ Route 113A off of Route 113 at North Sandwich. Route 113A rejoins route 113.

Welcome

Province Lake

Route 153 is a narrow road. Although it has an occasional bumpy part, the ride generally hugs the land over hills and around the lakes. It features very little traffic. This is a riding road, with few villages to disturb your ride. Watch the road signs to be warned of surprise 90-degree turns coming just over the crest of the small hill ahead (this happens a few times, so all the more fun). If you are tired, choose from a number of lakes to rest, the prettiest on Route 153 being **Province Lake.**

Mount Chocorua dominates the area around Province Lake. Mount Chocorua is named after the Indian chief Chocorua who, according to popular legend, was friendly to the white settlers and befriended in particular a family named Campbell. Leaving on a hunting expedition, Chocorua left his motherless son with the Campbells for safekeeping. The Campbells, being harassed by some wolves, made a poison which Chocorua's son swallowed accidentally and died. Chocorua, on his return, could not accept the death as an accident. He killed the Campbells. Hunted by the other settlers, Chocorua was shot, climbed the mountain and leapt to his death, cursing the white man with his final breath.

The small towns along Route 153 offer diner-type ambiance. The **Poor People's Pub,** in downtown Sanbornville, is a "cheap eats" lunch and supper place, with five-dollar pitchers of cold drinks, homemade soups, desserts, and pub grub. There are always a couple of steeds parked outside.

Route 153 intersects with Route 75 after crossing Route 16. Route 75 and a rather commercial Highway 11 are there only to get you from Route 153 to Route 140. If you see a sign that says OLD ROUTE 11, ignore it!

Route 140 is a great road with little traffic, and good curves where your skill determines your speed level. The driving is in the 35 to 60 MPH range. This route leads eventually to Route 132, a delightful surprise that ripples and plays tag with Interstate 93. While all those cars are heading straight north, you're playing peek-a-boo with them. Route 132 was recently paved, and I'm sure there are places to pull over, but I didn't want to take my eyes off the road or break the rhythm of me and my steed doing the 132-step.

By the end of Route 132, which merges with Route 3, my mind was smoking and I figured, "Oh good, a chance to catch my breath," but nooo. Just before **Squam Lake** in Holderness, a freshly paved Route 113 begins.

On Golden Pond

Squam Lake is where they filmed the movie "On Golden Pond." You can get homemade ice cream at the Squam Lakeside Farm, a large barn opposite the lake. I found it a good stopping place, especially for an ice cream meister like myself. The traffic is a little thick right there, but thins out in a hurry.

Route 113 redefines the word "smooth" in the context of road feel. It might also have been the quietness created by my ears being blocked from a long twisting ascent. The climb, after leaving Squam Lake, up Route 113 east toward Mount Chocorua is an up, then slightly down, then up and around love affair with the transition from lake to mountain. This road has more curves than a day's worth of hour glasses. The engineer must have been a descendant of the Sidewinder family. Speed will definitely dictate the amount of challenge this terrain has to offer. Your ability to accelerate out of and decelerate into these rapid curves smoothly and safely is a measure of your skill. Passing through Center Sandwich, N.H., on your left you'll see an earthen road which crosses Sandwich Notch. Count it as a viewing but not a crossing. You will see enough notches on this journey that you don't need to sacrifice the steed on this one.

If you still have the time or inclination to extend the ride, branch off of Route 113 to Route 113A.

Route 113A is as curvy as Route 113, but is less used. The road is tighter and narrower than Route 113 at this point, a little more bumpy too, but avoids a couple of small towns. Route 113A reconnects with Route 113 at Tamworth, N.H.

Route 113 intersects with Route 16. At Chocorua follow it south to home base.

A remote Route 113, Sandwich, N.H.

New England at its finest

The Western Notches Loop

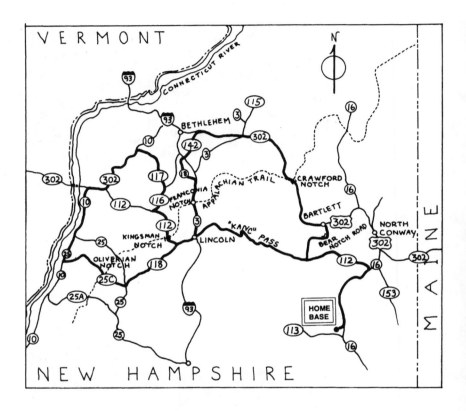

The Western Notches Loop

· ·

Distance   *210 miles (336 kilometers)*
Speed   *20 to 60 MPH (33 to 100 KPH)*
Highlights   *Highway to rural, ascents to river runs, famed tourist attractions*

The Route from White Lake State Park

→ Route 16 north to Route 112 west (Kancamagus Highway) just south of Conway, N.H.
→ Route 112 west, then right on to Bear Notch Road (heading north).
→ Bear Notch Road north to Route 302 west at Bartlett.
→ Route 302 west to Route 142 south at Bethlehem.
→ Route 142 south to Route 18 south at junction.
→ Route 18 south to Interstate 93/Route 3 south at junction.
→ Interstate 93/Route 3 south to Route 3 south at "The Flume" exit.
→ Route 3 south to Route 112 west at North Woodstock.
→ Route 112 west to Route 118 west at junction.*
→ Route 118 west to Route 25C west at Warren.
→ Route 25C west to Route 10 north at Piermont.
→ Route 10 north to Route 302 east at junction.
→ Route 302 east to Route 117 south at junction.
→ Route 117 south to Route 116 south at junction.
→ Route 116 south to Route 112 east at junction.
→ Route 112 east to Route 16 south at junction. To home base.

* Alternate route:

→ If you want to shorten the trip by 38 miles, stay on Route 112 west to 302 east. Skip the 118-to-25C-to-10 loop.

This loop includes some of the best-known attractions in the region and the most notches crossed in the White Mountain journey. Prepare for a long day if you want to catch all the attractions, since the major attractions are usually crowded, although the facilities seem to manage the flow well. I built in opportunities to reduce the ride, depending on your sightseeing preferences.

Route 112 is the Kancamagus Highway (locals call it "the Kanc," pronounced like crank without the r). Off of Route 16, it is a prelude for the day's ride. Sometimes crowded, the Kancamagus is a nationally renowned scenic highway. The road follows the Swift River for approximately 20 miles. About 14 miles up the Kancamagus is Bear Notch Road and the first notch of the loop. The nine-mile drive north on Bear Notch Road offers outlooks to Crawford Notch, Mount Washington, and the Carter Range. The Western Loop returns to the Kancamagus from the west later on.

Bear Notch Road feeds into Route 302, which is an ascent road to Crawford Notch. The road is wide with passing lanes, so the traffic is not a bother. Stop in the Appalachian Mountain Club (AMC) information hut, which was built in 1891 as a railroad station for the Maine Central Railway.

The old railroad station at Crawford Notch State Park, now an information center for the Appalachian Mountain Club

Out in the wilderness, the fabulous Mount Washington Hotel

You can get postcards offering unusual shots of the area attractions and read the posted weather information from the top of Mount Washington. Across the parking lot, the Appalachian Trail intersects with Route 302. This junction of road and trail brings together people from many backgrounds, all sharing the raw beauty. It is a great people-watching 20-minute coffee break.

Back on Route 302, the road tends to flatten at the summit. About 4 miles up the road, the Mount Washington Hotel comes into view. This elaborate White Mountain hotel is in the tradition of the grand hotels popular in the 1920s and 1930s. This particular hotel was the site of the famous 1944 Bretton Woods Economic Summit, which established the International Monetary Fund and World Bank.

The route to the Franconia Notch Parkway from Route 142 to Route 18 to Interstate 93 is small roads through a couple of ski areas and their respective complement of bars, restaurants, and attractions. Franconia Notch Parkway, cutting through the Franconia Notch State Park, holds the main events in the area for tourists. The natural phenomena of the **Flume, Old Man of the Mountain,** and the **Cannon Mountain Tramway** are

Entering Franconia Notch State Park, with Cannon Mountain ski area in the distance

natural tourist magnets, exploited to the hilt. It's worth going through and to; I just want to set your expectations for the six miles (Smokies are everywhere).

Whew! Once you make it through the Franconia Notch gauntlet, open up the throttle, accelerate out of the attractions, and head straight into the curves of our original objective. All the "100" routes (Routes 112, 116, 117, and 118) are joys to ride—twisting and turning like Chubby Checker on a cheap vibrator bed, no quarters needed! You can add two more notches to your belt along the way, too. The Oliverian Notch can be seen from Route 25C just over Lake Tarlton. Route 112 west to Route 118 south to Route 25C gets you there.

Route 10, like most major north-south roads, follows a river (the Connecticut). Unlike most river roads, which travel the floor of the valley, Route 10 sits high up, with gentle farmland fields flowing down to the river banks. This reminds me more of Vermont terrain than of New Hampshire; in fact, the opposite shore line

Oliverian Notch

is Vermont. Where Route 10 north joins Route 302 east, you start to veer away from the river.

About 11 miles up Route 10/302, you intersect with Route 117. This is a lazy road of forest and hills. When you reach the town of Sugar Hill, slow down and look for **Sunset Hill Road.** It doesn't matter what time of day it is; the 1,500-foot elevation atop Sugar Hill makes the view one of the sweetest. If you want to blow your budget, make reservations for the Sunset Hill House. Its rooms overlooking the Presidential Range and its country French cuisine will make for a lifelong memory.

Just after Sunset Hill on Route 117 is **Polly's Pancake Parlor.** If, like me, you're a firm believer that breakfast is the most important meal of the day, regardless of the hour, Polly's is a must on your list. The "parlor" was built in 1830 as the carriage shed and later wood shed to the Hildex Maple Sugar Farm. During the Depression, Polly and Wilfred (Sugar Bill) Dexter began serving "all you can eat" pancakes and waffles for fifty cents. Sixty years later, the family still lives at and manages the farm and Parlor. All the mixes are made from scratch and include whole wheat, buckwheat, oatmeal buttermilk and cornmeal pancakes. The grains are organically grown and are stone ground by the proprietors. Their forte though, is maple products, which are toppings for the fare.

If you can move after breakfast (did I mention the cob-smoked bacon?), rejoin Route 117, which merges with Route 116 south. These roads bring you straight (figuratively, not literally) back to Route 112. Route 112, west of Interstate 93, parallels the wild Ammonoosuc River and is a much less traveled road than the Kancamagus Highway, which is the east side of Route 112. The Kingsman Notch is on Route 112 heading east, just before North Woodstock, N.H.

When you cross Interstate 93 in the town of Lincoln, the Kancamagus begins. There are many scenic vista parking areas, and Kancamagus Pass could be your sixth notch of the loop except for the nomenclature. The Kancamagus Highway leads you back to Route 16 south to home base. The road would be perfect if not for the traffic. Do not attempt this road on a fall weekend unless you have the need to frustrate yourself as part of an obscure ritual of masochism. The spectacular fall foliage does nothing to make up for hours of breathing bumper-to-bumper exhaust fumes.

The view from Sugar Hill is sweet

The Kancamagus Highway, a bit of the Alps in New Hampshire

The North Country Notches Loop

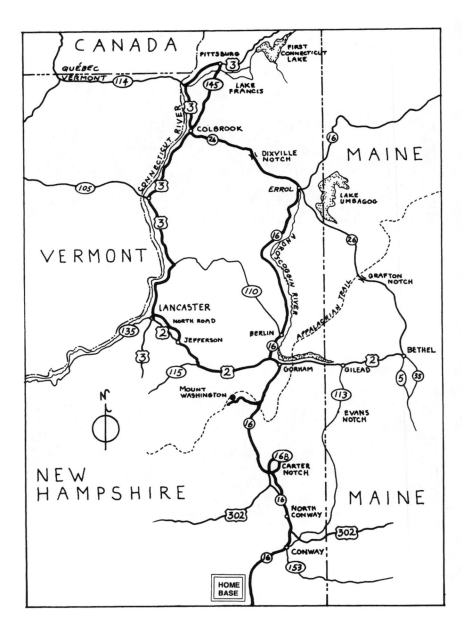

The North Country Notches Loop

· ·

Distance *230 miles (368 kilometers)*

Speed *5 to 65* MPH *(8 to 108* KPH*)*

Highlights *Dramatic scenery, mountain climbs, sweeping river road curves*

The Route from White Lake State Park

→ Route 16 north to Jackson, N.H.

→ Route 16B north from Jackson to Carter Notch.
   NOTE: Route 16B forms a loop north of Jackson.

→ Return on Route 16B back to Route 16 north.

→ Route 16 north to Mount Washington Auto Road.

→ Take the Mount Washington Auto Road to the summit and return by the same road.

→ Rejoin Route 16 north to Route 2 west at Gorham.

→ Route 2 west to North Road at Jefferson.

→ North Road to Route 2 west/Route 3 north at Lancaster..

→ Route 3 north to Route 145 south at Pittsburg.

→ Route 145 south to Route 26 east at Colebrook.

→ Route 26 east to Route 16 south at Errol.

→ Route 16 south to home base.

Start out from White Lake State Park, through North Conway on Route 16. Crossing Route 302, you start to feel, not just see, the high country. About a mile north of the Route 302 intersection (in Glen) are signs for Jackson. Take the Route 16B loop for your first notch of the day, Carter Notch.

Turn around and return to Route 16, heading north. The Presidential Range, sometimes referred to as the "Ridgepole of New England," starts to loom larger and larger off to the west.

The drama builds as you cross Pinkham Notch (add it to your collection); the full mountain range is at

Here we go

your feet. Mount Washington, the highest peak in the Northeast (elevation 6,288 feet), has some of the harshest weather in North America. In fact, the highest wind ever recorded was measured at 237 MPH in the 1938 hurricane, on the summit. There is plant life at the summit that only thrives in arctic conditions. And . . . you can get to the summit via the **Mount Washington Auto Road.**

Bikes are $6.00. I approached the toll booth with a mixture of apprehension and excitement. The ranger was just changing the weather board to up the wind gust velocity to 60 MPH. I asked him what the story was. He said "Motorcycles are allowed up as long as the wind gusts stay below 65 MPH."

I said, "They're supposed to diminish to 15 to 30 MPH tomorrow. I'll come back."

"This is one of the best days of the year, with visibility over 100 miles," he replied, like any good salesperson. I turned around, deciding the weather was predicted to be the same the next day with the winds lowering. About three miles up Route 16, agonizing over my decision, I changed my mind. In my travels I have been more pleasantly surprised by taking the risk, so *carpe diem* (seize the day)!

"This bike climbed Mt. Washington."

"Back again? It's only gusting to 60, averaging 35," said the ranger as I paid my $6.00, and received my THIS BIKE CLIMBED MT. WASHINGTON bike-sized bumper sticker. This was a good omen and confidence builder. The ranger thought I'd be successful!

The beginning was simple enough: the road was paved, wooded on both sides, and immediately started a steep climb. The signs on the descent side of the road before each pulloff stated "cool brakes frequently." The degree of climb I was experiencing made me understand why 4-wheeled vehicles need to make frequent

*"Boys on one side,
girls on the other."*

stops on the descent. The steed felt comfortable in second gear until I broke the tree line.

The road alternated between roadbed and pavement from the tree line to the summit. The switchbacks and vistas caused me to alternate between first and second for the second four miles of the eight-mile climb. Halfway up, I decided it would be better to do my rubbernecking on the way down with the views and road in front of me. I had a car a few hundred yards ahead of me and wanted to keep that buffer, not only

The Presidential Range, seen from Mt. Washington

for safety reasons, but to make my ride steadier for not having to adjust to the pace of the car.

At the summit, I pulled up next to five Harleys. They seemed to stake out a comfortable parking zone. Everywhere I turned was a photo opportunity, and this was just the parking lot!

I climbed the stairs to "Tip Top Hill." The structure on it, the "Tip Top House," used to be a hotel in 1853 when you could only get to the summit by climbing. The hotel failed, though, and the Tip Top House became the publishing offices of the "Among The Clouds" newspaper until 1915. The carriage road was completed in 1861 and the Mount Washington Cog Railroad was completed in 1869. The railroad's coal-fired steam engine still climbs its 37-degree track—the second steepest in the world—on daily trips out of Bretton Woods. Most of the track is laid on wooden trestles.

The descent was all I anticipated. First gear the whole way; I hardly had to apply the brakes. The view is unrivaled and the ride deliciously slow.

I recommend the trip if the weather cooperates, which happens only a few precious days a year. *Carpe diem.*

It ain't Amtrak

Rejoining Route 16 north in my invigorated state, I headed for the northern reaches of the White Mountains. Because of its proximity to the Appalachian Trail, and the Presidential Range, Gorham, at the junction of Routes 2 and 16, is popular with hikers, bikers, and outdoor sports people. You can choose from a variety of motels, campgrounds, small inns and restaurants if you want to move home base farther north.

The virtually unknown and unused Jericho State Park in Berlin, about 6 miles north on 16 from Gorham, has only five campsites, all on the lake. It is used by the locals for the public beach and has a bath house with hot showers, etc. It is only attended from 10 a.m. to 4 p.m. I arrived after 4 and left the next morning before 10. The place has lovely sunsets over the lake with silhouettes of the Crescent Mountains.

Route 2 west out of Gorham is a wide, smooth two-laner with easy passing. Just after Jefferson, take North Road, the first right turn after the junction of

Spectacular Mt. Washington Valley

Route 116 and Route 2 on your left. This is an alternative to staying on Route 2 to Lancaster. North Road is more rural with less traffic and more twisties.

Grab Route 3 north in Lancaster. Route 3 is a truck route until you get above Colebrook; however, it does parallel the Connecticut River from Lancaster to its headwaters in West Stewartstown, providing valley scenery. The **Northumberland Diner** on Route 3, about eight miles out of Lancaster in the town of the same name, is a good place to get fresh baked goods with breakfast. The signpost outside says DOUBLE SS DINER, which I thought stood for the two sisters inside, but is the previous name (I don't know if the sign will be up or down by the time you read this so I give you both). The food is a cut above the standard fare, the bantering from the owners and staff is fodder for your stories, and the education I received on moose safety showed a genuine concern for strangers. I defy you to find a chef

*May the force be
with you!*

in New England, behind the grill, who better comple-
ments her Harley tee. Be discreet, please!

On Route 3 just before Colebrook is the **Shrine of
our Lady of Grace.** This is a large shrine depicting the
birth of Christ. It is also the site of an annual blessing of
motorcycle riders. Thousands of bikes gather here each
year in the middle of June to be blessed. The White
Mountain Riders Motorcycle Club is host to the annual
gathering.

As you can see from the picture, this may be the
only memorial to two-wheelers. It's the only one I've
seen. If you know of any others, let me know.

Return to Route 3 north after the shrine. Above
Colebrook the road becomes far more narrow and interesting to ride. You intersect with Route 145 in Pittsburg,
and cross the 45th parallel (halfway between the North
Pole and the equator) just south of town. At 360 square
miles, Pittsburg has the distinction of being the biggest
town east of the Mississippi. If you haven't seen Bull-
winkle or any of his brethren yet and want to, stay on
Route 3 north past First Connecticut Lake. Watch the
marshy areas. If you see parked cars, they are probably
watching moose.

The Balsams

The formal garden at the Balsams

Take Route 145 south back to Colebrook to Route 26 east. Get ready for Dixville Notch and **The Balsams.**

Just opposite Dixville Notch, The Balsams is a grand old New Hampshire resort, similar to the Mount Washington Hotel, billed as the Switzerland of the U.S. I always pull in for something cold to drink, and a rest. I'd suggest it to be the final stop but $250 a day is pretty steep. The guests here are usually three generations deep; whole families come here for a week at a time. The surroundings and environment are something to relish. It is wonderful to stroll the grounds overlooking the lake and the Notch.

Late afternoon on the veranda can bring sumptuous hors d'oeuvres, like fresh strawberries and chocolate for dipping—no charge for guests, of course. The Balsams is a legend which you can enjoy now.

Back on Route 26, the road climbs through Dixville Notch to Route 16. Route 16 south from Errol follows every bend in the Androscoggin River, exposing pristine land, marsh, and river bank. The only interruption is an occasional canoe or angler in the river.

The **13 Mile Woods** scenic area is a favorite with local bikers because of the turns, isolation, and remoteness. I chose to incorporate this run into the Northeast Loop as well as this one. You are hardly disturbed traveling this thirty mile stretch of road from Errol except by your own imagination . . . until you reach Berlin (pronounced BER-lin).

Berlin is dominated physically, economically, and socially by the James River Corporation. Its mill there makes paper and paper products. The physical presence is awesome, yet incongruous with the mountains in the background. I saw the paper mill from Mount Washington, although at the time I didn't realize what it was; it dominated the valley even from that perspective. It's the only work in town. Stay upwind if you can! Paper is one of the largest polluting industries we have, and it smells it. Route 16 back to home base is a straight shot.

Nirvana

The Northeast Notches Loop

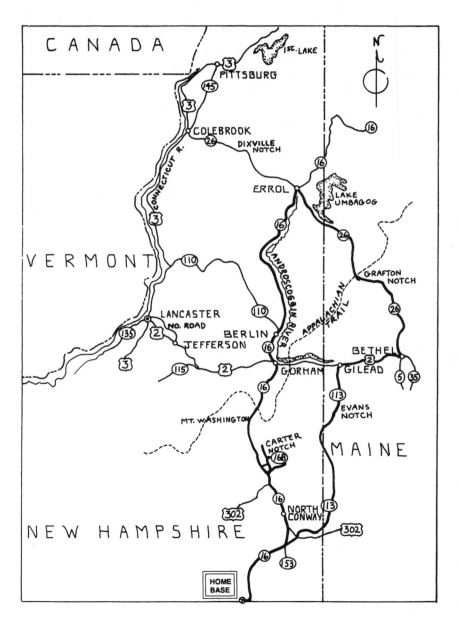

The Northeast Notches Loop

Distance	*200 miles (320 kilometers)*
Speed	*15 to 65* MPH *(24 to 108* KPH*)*
Highlights	*River roads and scenic stops, an easy high country route*

The Route from White Lake State Park

→ Route 16 north to Route 26 east at Errol.

→ Route 26 east to Route 2 west at Bethel, Maine.

→ Route 2 west to Route 113 south at Gilead, Maine.

→ Route 113 south to Route 16 south at Conway, N.H.

→ Route 16 south to White Lake State Park.

This is a simple route that provides an easy outing with plenty of scenery. Route 16 is worthwhile from both directions. Going north this time, you travel upstream with better views of the Adroscoggin River.

The day I rode north, I came upon three deer in the road. As I slowed, they broke for the woods. I decided to pull over and see if they would return if I was real

Huggin' the Androscoggin River

*Around the world
in eight years*

still. While I was waiting, a bicyclist in full road gear came by heading south. I called to him about the deer. He pulled over for a chat.

The gentleman had silver hair and a well tanned road-worn face. There was a uniqueness about him that was hard to place. I asked him where he was going, and he said "North Conway." I asked him where he was coming from, and he smiled. It turned out he was re-turning from an *eight-year circumnavigation of the world by bicycle.* He began his odyssey in 1983 and on this day he was going to make home. I was startled. I had to restrain myself from asking a million inane questions. Being on the road for only months at a time, I had to ask him what the toughest part of his travel was. He said it was struggling with the loneliness for the first five years. Bicycling is a solitary mode of transportation. I could relate but ever so slightly. In the end, he had his mission and I had mine, and off we went in separate directions, I a little less lonely for the camaraderie of aloneness.

At the intersection of Routes 16 and 26 at Errol, hang a right and go east into Maine. You will see a lot of Canadian license plates, for this is one of the routes to Old Orchard Beach from Montreal. Old Orchard Beach is a large Quebecois hangout.

Just after you enter the Grafton Notch State Park, you will find a number of waterfalls, swimming holes and picnic areas throughout the park, so grab some food back in Upton.

From Newry on Route 26 to Gilead on Route 2, the roadside gets more traveled and commercial. This stretch of commercialism is a small price to pay for getting to Route 113 south, a special road through **Evans Notch State Park.**

This is a narrow, smooth and winding road that climbs to Evans Notch. The signs that warn you to watch out for logging trucks seem appropriate. Although I did not encounter any, I can't imagine one fitting on just their half of this asphalt alley. Without trucks and traffic, this road is a genuine find.

After Evans Notch, it's back to Conway and the short scoot home on Route 16.

Honesty is the best policy

Places of Interest

∙∙∙

NEW HAMPSHIRE

Colebrook Shrine of Our Lady of Grace, Route 3. Phone (603) 237-5511 for information on the blessing of the motorcycles. Motorcycle heaven, literally. There is no charge for visiting the Shrine.

Dixville Notch The Balsams, Route 26. Phone (800) 255-0600. Daily, year-round. A little bit of the Alps in America. Beautiful scenery, and luxury. A legend in its own time. $$$

Franconia New England Ski Museum, Franconia Notch State Park. Phone (603) 823-7177. Daily 9:00 a.m. to 5:00 p.m. Open May to October, and ski season if you put the spikes on the treads. If you are an enthusiast, videos and a history of how we evolved from barrel slats. $$

Robert Frost Place, Ridge Road. Phone (603) 823-8038. Daily 10:00 a.m. to 5:00 p.m. Open Memorial day to Columbus Day. Frost's farmhouse restored as a museum. $

North Conway Mount Washington Valley Theater Company, Eastern Slope Playhouse, Route 16. Phone (603) 356-5701. Call for schedule; if you are in town and something is going on, try to get tickets for the evening performances. Fun summer theater without the pretense of regular theater-goers. $$

Northumberland Northumberland Diner, Route 3. Phone (603) 636-2831. Daily 5:00 a.m. to 8:00 p.m. Open year-round. Fresh baked muffins, nice buns, too. $

Pinkham Notch Mount Washington Auto Road, Route 16. Phone (603) 466-3988. 7:30 a.m. to 6:00 p.m. $6.00. Weather permitting, it's a tale to tell!!!

Sanbornville Poor People's Pub, Main Street. Phone (603) 522-8378. Daily 11:00 a.m. to 11:00 p.m., opens Sunday at noon. Year-round good pub grub. Always a couple of steeds outside. $$

Sugar Hill Polly's Pancake Parlor, Route 117. Phone (603) 823-5575. Daily 7:00 a.m. to 3:00 p.m., weekends till 7:00 p.m. Late April through late October. The best! $$

Sunset Hill House, Sunset Hill Rd. Phone (603) 823-5522. Daily year-round inn. For the view, if not for the inn, get there before sunset! $$$

Tamworth White Lake State Park, Route 16. Phone (603) 323-7350. Late May through Columbus Day. First come, first served. On White Lake, swimming along with the other normal facilities. Well kept and centrally located. $12.00 per campsite.

Travel Information

· ·

NEW HAMPSHIRE

Automated Teller Machines
Phone (800) 523-4175, fast cash locations 24 hrs.

Mount Washington Valley Chamber of Commerce
P.O. Box 385, North Conway, N.H. 03860. Phone (603) 356-3171.

New Hampshire Office of Vacation Travel
P.O. Box 856, Concord, N.H. 03301. Phone (603) 846-2666 for New Hampshire tourist map. Good information on state parks, attractions and even automatic teller locations.

Traditional B & B Association of N.H.
83 Old Lake Shore Rd., Gilford, N.H. 03246. Phone (603) 528-1172.

White Mountains Attractions
Phone (800) FIND MTS.

Emergency and Medical Assistance

NEW HAMPSHIRE

Colebrook   Upper Connecticut Valley Hospital, Corliss Lane. Phone (603) 237-4971.

Laconia   Lakes Region General Hospital, Highland Street. Phone (603) 524-3211.

Littleton   Littleton Regional Hospital, 107 Cottage Street. Phone (603) 444-7731.

North Conway   North Conway Memorial Hospital, Intervale Road. Phone (603) 356-7421.

Wolfeboro   Huggins Hospital, So. Main Street. Phone (603) 569-2150.

State Police   Emergencies Phone (800) 525-5555.

Until next time

Closing the Green Mountain Gaps

The Green Mountain Gaps are a natural extension of either the Lakes Journey or the Berkshires Journey. Southeast of Lake Champlain, and due north of the Berkshires, the two loops of this journey crisscross the Green Mountain National Forest. The Long Trail, a 270-mile primitive footpath that inspired the Appalachian Trail, follows the central ridge of the Green Mountains and bisects our Green Mountain Gap Loops. The southern portion of the Long Trail, coinciding with the Appalachian Trail in the Berkshires, is the oldest long-distance footpath in the United States and contains some of the steepest, most rugged climbs in the Northeast.

Where the other journeys may be thought of as marathons, this mountain climb to valley to mountain crest journey is a wind sprint. In a relatively compact space of 350 miles, if you consolidate the two loops (shall we call it a loop-de-loop), you will tame five gaps, twice. The fun of crossing these gaps twice is the distinctly different terrain on each side of the mountain.

For example, going west across the Lincoln Gap, the east side is a two mile ascent complete with sharp turns, hairpins and ridge views on your right near the crest. Crossing the gap, the descent on the west side is very steep, very short, and straight through a stand of pine, with a dirt roadbed to greet you at the bottom.

Going east, the west side of Lincoln Gap is the steepest climb I encountered in Vermont, while the east

*Adjoining paths in
the wilderness*

side provides a long second gear descent and a view of the valley. The road provides two entirely different challenges. All the gaps are like this, with one side being sharp and steep and the other a long, luxurious climb.

Therefore, by shooting the gaps from both directions over the two-loop journey, you don't have to keep one eye on the rear view mirror and one eye on the road.

Since you'll be passing many of the highlighted places of interest more than once, you may not always reach them at an appropriate time to stop. For example, you will pass Texas Falls, a small, remote picnic area and trail on Route 125, in the early morning on the Southern Gap Loop and in the afternoon on the Northern Gap Loop. Where you would have a tendency not to stop within the first 30 miles of the day, at the 100

Home base, Branbury State Park

mile mark, at mid-day, it is perfect. The first time you pass a place of interest I will highlight it; however, I will remind you at the more appropriate time on either loop.

Home base for this journey is **Branbury State Park** at the east end of 1,035-acre Lake Dunmore in Brandon, Vermont. In addition to 42 campsites, mostly nestled in the woods against a steep hillside, the park has a large beach (crowded on summer weekends) for that early morning swim or late evening dip after a hard day's ride. In early fall, you will probably be the only one there.

The Southern Gap Loop

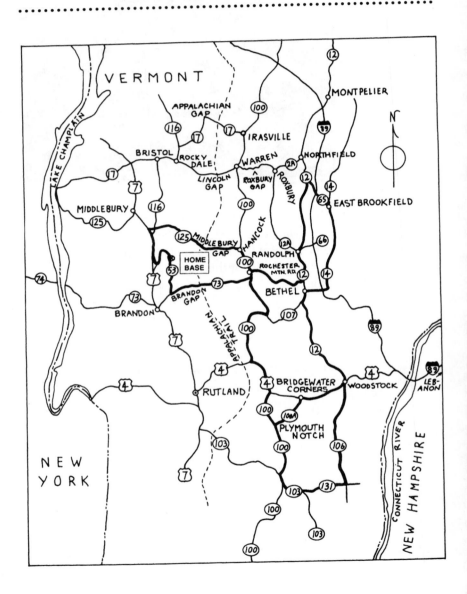

The Southern Gap Loop

Distance	*158 miles (253 kilometers)*
Speed	*10 to 55* MPH *(16 to 88* KPH*)*
Highlights	*Over mountains, through forests, around lakes and down river valley roads*

The Route from Branbury State Park

→ Vermont Route 53 north to Route 7 north at junction.

→ Route 7 north to Route 125 east at East Middlebury, Vt.

→ Route 125 east to Rte. 100 south at Hancock.*

→ Route 100 south to Route 100A north at Plymouth Union.

→ Route 100A north to Route 4 east at Bridgewater Corners.

→ Route 4 east to Route 12 north at Woodstock.

→ Route 12 north to Route 107 east at junction.

→ Route 107 east to Route 14 north at junction.

→ Route 14 north to Route 65 west at junction above East Brookfield.

→ Route 65 west to Route 12 south at junction.

→ Route 12 south to Rochester Mountain Road at junction.

→ Rochester Mountain Road west to Route 100 south at Rochester.

→ Route 100 south to Route 73 west at junction.

→ Route 73 west to Route 53 north at Forest Dale.

* Trip Extension

For an additional 40 miles:

→ Stay on Route 100 south to Route 103 east at Ludlow.

→ Route 103 east to Rte 131 east at Proctorsville.

→ Route 131 east to Rte 106 north at Downers.

→ Route 106 north to Route 12 north at Woodstock.

Old Hancock Hotel

Route 53 is a small lake road typical of access roads to summer cottages everywhere. Route 125, a major east-west route across the Green Mountain National Forest, presents the longer climb going east, crossing Middle-bury Gap (2,149 feet) at about the 11-mile mark of the 16 miles between Routes 7 and 100.

Route 125 is also named the Robert Frost Memorial Highway. The poet, a long-time resident of the area, lived in a small cabin using the solitude of the sur-roundings to recharge his batteries after long winter tours. Just before a picnic area on the south side of the road is the **Robert Frost Interpretive Trail,** a one-mile walking trail with the wilderness scenes that inspired Frost and the corresponding poems—a place to ponder or impress your friends with your new literary prowess ("And miles to go before I sleep, and miles to go before I sleep.").

After the Robert Frost Trail, through Middlebury Gap, the road begins a quick, steep descent. The **Texas Falls** (it is clearly marked), on the north side, a half-mile up a small road, are a great place to stretch your legs, have a picnic, or just relax.

The **Old Hancock Hotel** at the corner of Route 125 and Route 100 is an excellent local eating spot. Dating from the mid-1800s, it's home to good food at reasonable prices, with some culinary mountain treasures. The cob-smoked bacon for breakfast or the cob-smoked ham for lunch "to go" offer an unexpected sweet-smoked full flavor. The same corn cobs you know from those old pipes are burned to flavor this creation. Specials are always offered at the counter, at the tables, or to go for porch dining. I got sandwiches to go and ran up to Texas Falls.

Route 100 south is a long valley road that parallels the White River. Typical of valley roads, the curves on Route 100 are long and sweeping, with plenty of scenery and views of the upcoming turns. Route 100, a popular alternative to Interstate 89, runs from the southern border of Vermont to the Canadian border, a lazy rider's run through some very pretty country.

You touch the southern origins of Route 100, off Route 112 north, in the Berkshires Journey. Perhaps you'll decide to connect the two journeys.

Route 100A north, an extension of Route 100, passes Calvin Coolidge's birthplace in Plymouth Notch, a humble beginning—and end—for the 30th President of the United States. Five generations of his forebears are buried with him on a terraced hillside.

Robert Frost Highway, Route 125, Hancock, Vermont

*Floating Bridge at
East Brookfield*

Route 4 follows the Ottauquechee River east to Woodstock. This Woodstock, unlike its famous relative in New York, is supported by the Rockefellers and is an upscale town of stately inns and ivy-covered brick.

Routes 12, 107, and 14 are winding roads following the paths laid eons ago by the river beds they follow. They bring you to Route 65 and a unique structure, aptly named the **Floating Bridge,** a wooden bridge that crosses Sunset Lake by literally floating on its surface. Stay on the wooden tire tracks! The water seeps through the wooden roadbed, almost to the level of the tracks, as the weight of you and your steed sink the bridge into the lake surface. On the north side of the east end of the bridge is **Hippopotamus Park.** There resides a small white granite sculpture of two hippos, entitled *Father & Son,* created by Jim Sardonis. The granite comes from Bethel, Vermont, just south on the interstate. Route 65 west of the Floating Bridge turns to dirt roadbed for about 2½ miles, just after cresting the west side of Sunset Lake. The dirt surface is hard-packed, but be careful of the ruts created by rain runoff. It can feel like a metal-decked bridge if you get into them.

At the T, take a left. This is still Route 65, but there are no signs at that intersection. The signs for Route 65 west begin again about a quarter-mile down the road from the T. At the junction, the road turns back to asphalt.

A side trip off Route 12 south, onto Route 66 east just out of Randolph and before the intersection of Interstate 89, will bring you to an incongruous mountain scene: *Reverence*, another sculpture by Jim Sardonis. It is a celebration of the environment: twin whale flukes of African granite, on a hillside overlooking the mountains, hundreds of miles from their watery habitat. Originally named *Pas De Deux*, a dance for two, the concept came to Jim in a dream. Each tail is made from two blocks of granite, and is there to remind us of the interconnection of all species, near and far.

Back on Route 12 south, take Rochester Mountain

Whales tales

*Coming over
Roxbury Mountain*

Road, your second right, at a small street sign saying ROCHESTER with an arrow. This begins a 25-mile stretch west across two mountains. The ten miles over Rochester Mountain are a real treat, a diamond no longer in the rough. While all the road maps show an unpaved road across the top, it is, in fact, freshly paved. There is no traffic other than an occasional local. The 100-mile views from the top, surrounded by birches and pines, are a show stopper, and the climb is just the way we like 'em—long and curvy!

The ride on Route 100 south lasts about a mile before you reach Route 73 west, over Brandon Gap (elevation 2,170 feet) and takes you straight, figuratively speaking, into Brandon. The east-to-west climb is the longer ascent through Brandon Gap.

If you are hungry on either side of the loop, take Route 73 west past Route 53 to Brandon. **Patricia's Restaurant,** on Center Street, offers fine victuals for lunch and dinner. Next door, the **Sun Rise Harvest Bakery** makes daily goodies and fresh breads.

*Patricia's
Restaurant,
Brandon, Vermont*

The Higher Northern Gaps

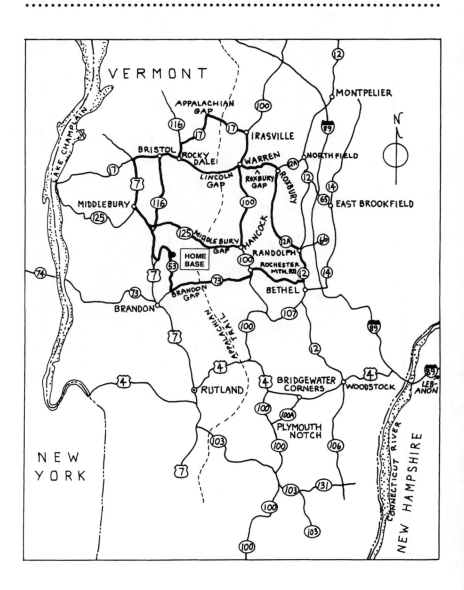

The Higher Northern Gaps

∙∙

Distance   *200 miles (320 kilometers)*

Speed   *5 to 55* MPH *(8 to 88* KPH*)*

Highlights   *Hairpins, mountain passages on a hard-pack dirt roadbed, scenic vistas, valley roads*

The Route from Branbury State Park

→ Route 53 south to Route 73 east at Forest Dale, Vt.

→ Route 73 east to Route 100 north at junction.

→ Route 100 north to Rochester Mountain Road at Rochester Common.

→ Rochester Mountain Road (follow signs to Bethel/Randolph) to Route 12 north at junction.

→ Route 12 north to Route 12A north at Randolph.

→ Route 12A north to Warren Mountain Road at Roxbury.

→ Warren Mountain Road to Route 100 south at junction.

→ Route 100 south to Lincoln Gap Road west. At the junction there is a sign TO LINCOLN.

→ Lincoln Gap Road west to Route 116 north at Rocky Dale junction.

→ Route 116 north to Route 17 east at junction.

→ Route 17 east to Route 100 south at Irasville.

→ Route 100 south to Route 125 west at Hancock.

→ Route 125 west to Route 7 north at junction.

→ Route 7 north to Route 17 east at New Haven Junction.

→ Route 17 to Lincoln Gap Road east (sign at junction says WARREN).

→ Lincoln Gap Rd. to Rte 100 north at junction.

→ Route 100 north to Route 17 west at Irasville.

→ Route 17 west to Route 116 south at junction.

→ Route 116 south to Route 7 south at East Middlebury.

→ Route 7 south to Route 53 south at junction.

We start out taking a 25-mile stretch of road east to Route 12. The west sides of the twin crossings are sharp, steep climbs with long third gear slopes on the backside. Route 12A is just a scoot paralleling the Third Branch White River to the town of Roxbury and Warren Mountain Road. These mountain roads change names depending on your direction. Therefore, the Warren Mountain Road turns into the Roxbury Mountain Road if you are heading eastward from Warren to Roxbury.

The road over Roxbury Gap is a hard packed dirt

Rochester Common

A view from the wooden bridge heading up to Lincoln Gap

roadbed for about five miles on either side of the gap. Just over the apex, off to the north side, is a pullover with a view that's worth the stop.

At a four-way intersection (left and right are paved, straight ahead is still dirt), take a left, following signs to Warren and Route 100 south out of Roxbury Gap and straight on through Lincoln Gap. In Warren, at the island, take a left past the post office on your right and the fire station on your left. About 100 yards up on the right is a old wooden bridge with an even older-looking hand-painted sign saying TO LINCOLN.

Go over the bridge and up the hill to Route 100. Diagonally across to the south is the road to Lincoln and Bristol, across Lincoln Gap.

The road changes to dirt and back to pavement twice. I stopped at the pulloff, which was easy to negotiate, and hiked a portion of the Long Trail to a clearing.

You can walk north or south from the Long Trail head at Lincoln Gap. The long expanse to the multiple peaks within the Green Mountains is awesome.

Route 116 north intersects with the road from Lincoln to Bristol at the end of a slow descent. That wistful feeling brought about by Lincoln Gap lingers until you

Lincoln Gap Road

grab Route 17 east, off of Route 116 north. It is the **McCullough Turnpike.**

Route 17 is the most challenging 16-mile stretch of road in Vermont. Hairpin turns come up without signage—90-degree stuff without warning. The road climbs with alpine dexterity to and through the Appalachian Gap at 2,356 feet. More than a few bikes run the McCullough Turnpike on Sundays. Stop at the small parking area, overlook a small lake where the Long Trail intersects, watch the bikes go by and peer westward for one of the most dramatic settings in the area. It is a road you will refer to whenever you play the game of OH YEAH, WELL HAVE YOU . . . !!

Route 100 at Irasville is just the road you need after the McCullough Turnpike's challenges. Like a race horse cooling down after the run, it meanders down Mad River to Route 125 west. Along the way are the Moss Glen Falls. Follow the signs for parking. Go across the small bridge and walk south; don't be fooled by the little waterfall at the bridge.

Route 125 west takes you past the Old Hancock Hotel at the corner and Texas Falls up the road, if you are inclined to take a break. Route 125 west, Route 7 north, and Route 17 east to Bristol twine among mountains, the upscale town of Middlebury (former capitol of Vermont), and valley roads.

Bristol is a friendly little village with a legend of lost treasure, said to be buried south of town on a mountainside known as Hell's Half Acre. According to the "Ballad of Old Pocock," Bristol's original name, Simeon Coreser raised a large sum of money to finance his lost treasure diggings. His chief surveyor was his private occultist. His partners, it is told, actually found treasure but Coreser ripped them off with a "field of schemes." The legend of buried treasure lives on, but is yet to be found in Hell's Half Acre.

In the town of Bristol itself is the **Bristol Bakery and Cafe,** where espresso and fresh baked goods satisfy even the most discriminating palate. The **Squirrel's Nest Restaurant** on Route 116, north of Bristol, is a family-style restaurant where quantity is never debated. Try the sesame chicken or the Big Barrel Break-

McCullough
Turnpike

NOT RECOMMENDED
FOR WINTER
TRAVEL BY
TRUCKS BUSSES
OR TRAILERS

Appalachian Gap,
McCullough
Turnpike

fast, depending on time of day and your appetite. I met a few tourers from Quebec here.

In the next forty miles you'll run the Lincoln Gap and the McCullough Turnpike in reverse. Just up the road from the Squirrel's Nest is the Lincoln Gap Road east to Lincoln and Warren. Returning to Route 100 north, take the McCullough Turnpike (Route 17) west to Route 116 south, through Bristol and back home.

Places of Interest

....

VERMONT

Brandon Patricia's Restaurant, 18 Center Street. Phone (802) 247-3223. Daily 11:00 a.m. to 9:00 p.m. Good burgers, soups and daily specials. $$

Sun Rise Harvest Bakery, 16 Center Street. Phone (802) 247-6047. Daily 7:00 a.m. to 2:00 p.m. Homemade baked goodies and coffee. $$

Bristol Bristol Bakery and Cafe, Route 116. Phone (802) 453-3280. Daily 7:00 a.m. to 1:00 p.m. Espresso, cinnamon twists, specials. YUM. $$$

The Squirrel's Nest Restaurant, Route 116. Phone (802) 453-6042. Daily, 5:00 a.m. to 9:00 p.m. Family dining. Say hi to Jay, the owner, before he says hi! Sesame chicken, Big Barrel Breakfast. $$

Hancock Old Hancock Hotel, Corner of Routes 100 & 125. No phone. Daily 7:00 a.m. to 8:00 p.m. Cob-smoked meats, down-home cooking. $$

Travel Information

VERMONT

Agency of Development & Commercial Affairs, Vermont Travel Division

134 State Street, Montpelier, 05601. Phone (802) 828-3236. Official State Guide & Touring Map, Vermont Vacation Guide, Country Inns, Annual Events Calendar, Traveler's Guidebook.

Branbury State Park

RFD #2, Brandon, 05733. Phone (802) 247-5925 or (802) 773-2733. Seven miles south on Route 7 from Middlebury, then three miles on Route 53 east.

Emergency and Medical Assistance

VERMONT

Berlin   Central Vermont Hospital, Fisher Road, Exit 7, I-89. Phone (802) 229-9121.

South Middlebury   Porter Medical Center, South Street. Phone (802) 388-7901.

Randolph   Gifford Memorial Hospital, 44 South Main Street. Phone (802) 728-3366.

Rutland   Rutland Regional Medical Center, 160 Allen Street. Phone (802) 775-7111.

State Police Barracks, Phone (802) 733-9101.

Waterbury   State Police Barracks. Phone (802) 244-7357.

Circumnavigating the Lakes

··

This journey encompasses the beauty and adventure of the three largest lakes—Champlain, George, and Placid—between the Adirondack and Green Mountain ranges. In fact, these lakes provided the geological mass for the mountain ranges, so long ago created by Ice Age glaciers. Many of the highlights in this chapter are geological in nature (no pun intended). This part of the Northeast offers challenging roads, historic places to visit, and natural scenery to enjoy.

I chose the Crown Point State Park in New York for home base. Sitting in view of the only bridge that crosses Lake Champlain, it afforded me an opportunity to be by the lake and easy access to Vermont. Stay in the lean-to. The lake is down a steep embankment in front of the lean-to that leads to a very private flat rock beach. Otherwise the campground is fairly open.

Home base: a lean-to at Crown Point State Park, N.Y.

The Lake George Loop

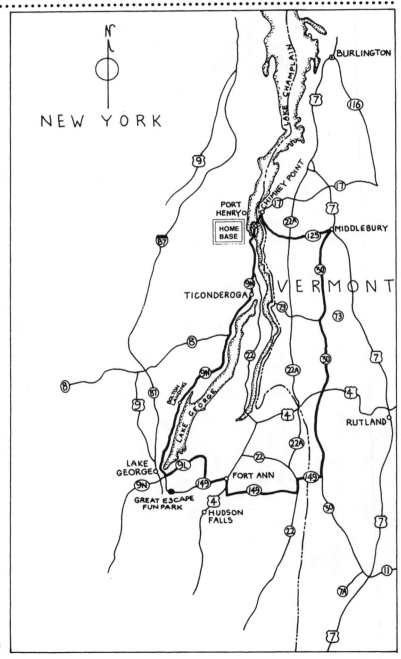

The Lake George Loop

· ·

Distance   *150 miles (240 kilometers)*

Speed   *35 to 60* MPH *(56 to 100* KPH*)*

Highlights   *Scenic with early curves*

The Route from Crown Point

→ Start at Crown Point State Park on the New York side (Chimney Point is on the Vermont side).

→ Take a left (heading west, away from Lake Champlain) to N.Y. Route 9N south.

→ Route 9N south to Route 9L east at junction.

→ Route 9L east to Route 149 east between Glens Falls and Fort Ann.

→ Route 149 east to Vt. Route 30 north.

→ Route 30 north to Route 125 west at Middlebury, Vt.

→ Route 125 west to Crown Point State Park (the signs say BRIDGE TO NEW YORK).

The run out of the campground to **Fort Ticonderoga** is short and a taste of what is to come on Route 9N. Stop at the fort. It has been completely restored, and is a delight for Revolutionary War buffs. The fort offers expansive views of both Lake Champlain and Lake George.

When you return to the center of town, follow signs to **Mt. Defiance.** It is a quick hill climb, but offers even more spectacular views of the lakes. With its guns facing down on Fort Ticonderoga, it gives you a feel for the battles that took place on the lake.

Between Ticonderoga and Bolton Landing, 9N really becomes an enjoyable test of your skills and brakes. The road hugs the lake shore like a glove, with the road as smooth as doeskin leather. It is better to travel this

Lake George, seen from Mt. Defiance

road mid-week and/or during fall and spring to best appreciate the ride it offers.

In Bolton Landing, stop at **Jules' Diner** (breakfast all day long, with a Mountain Man Special of eggs, meat, potatoes and all the trimmings). I stopped in the Chamber of Commerce for dining references when I arrived in Bolton Landing. Of the two people there, the older woman did the talking. She did not mention Jules'. It looked intriguing as I cruised by, though, so I decided to test it out. Not 20 minutes later, in strolled the other Chamber of Commerce attendant. Curious, I asked, "How come you didn't recommend Jules'?" He replied, "Jules' doesn't contribute so it does not get mentioned, but it is the best value around!" Jules' motto: "Good food, generous portions."

After Bolton Landing, the next 10 miles of 9N to Lake George and surroundings gets commercial. This is a touristy town with all the trappings, not that you mind getting trapped now and then. A different mode of seeing the town is by steamship out of the harbor. Some of the motels on the 9N strip will ferry their guests by boat to and from town (an indication of how bad summertime traffic can get).

The **Great Escape Fun Park** in Lake George is the largest amusement park in New York, with more than 100 rides and attractions. If you head up the east side of the lake, it gets a lot more rural (if you want to get away from town yet stay nearby). Branch off 9L east for Pilot Knobb and go to the end for a nice little picnic spot.

Return to 9L and pick up Route 149 and follow it to Vermont Route 30 north, which offers dramatic views of the Adirondacks on your left and the Green Mountains on your right. Rubbernecking is allowed because Route 30 is smooth and easy on both rider and driver all the way to Middlebury.

Middlebury is a college town with all the associated food, drink and resting places. **Woody's** is a good place to get some good food with a lively cross-section of the town. If you're into live steeds (if you bought this book I assume you are already into the iron variety), the Morgan Horse farm is just five miles north of town. Route 125 west out of town brings you back to the Crown Point campground.

Paddlewheelers on Lake George

The Lake Placid Loop

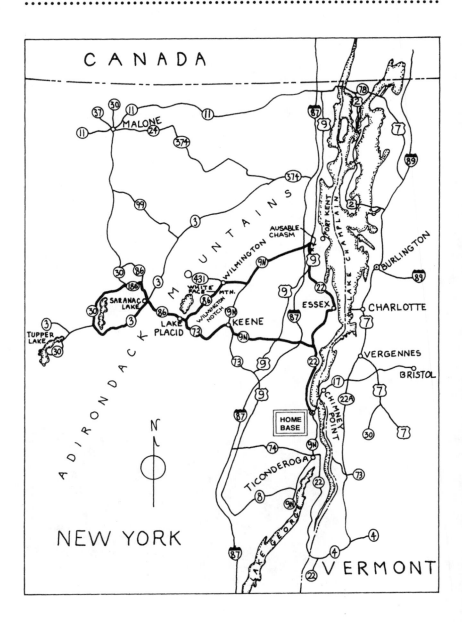

The Lake Placid Loop

· ·

Distance   *200 miles (320 kilometers)*

Speed   *15 to 65* MPH *(24 to 108* KPH*)*

Highlights   *Sharp curves, steep mountain climbs, lakes and ferry crossings*

The Route from Crown Point

→ Left out of the campground to N.Y. Route 22 north.

→ Route 22 north to route 9N west at Westport.

→ Route 9N west to Route 73 west, 2 miles south of Keene.

→ Route 73 west joins Route 86 in Lake Placid.

→ Route 86 west to Route 3 west at Saranac Lake.

→ Route 3 west to Route 30 north at junction.

→ Route 30 north to Route 186 east at Lake Clear Junction.

→ Route 186 east to Route 86 east at Harrietstown.

→ Route 86 east through Lake Placid to 9N east at Jay.

→ Route 9N east to Route 9 south at Ausable Chasm.

→ Route 9 south to Route 22 south about 7 miles south of Ausable Chasm.

→ Route 22 south to Crown Point State Park (BRIDGE TO VERMONT signs). *

* Alternate Route

→ Two ferry crossings offer alternate routes back to Crown Point State Park. For more information, see the route description.

This loop is high drama from the beginning run parallel to Lake Champlain, on through the climb into the Adirondacks, an outstanding loop around Saranac Lake, the conquering of Whiteface Mountain, and the piercing of Wilmington Notch. Route 22N north hugs Lake Champlain. If the air is hot you can experience the joys

The high peaks

of fog, as the lake remains cool through the early summer. Midsummer through fall, enjoy the views provided by the Green Mountains across the lake.

As soon as you pick up 9N out of Westport, you start to climb and climb and climb for the village of Lake Placid. Within a few miles, the lake is below and you are above it all.

These routes to Lake Placid were clearly designed to accommodate the rider through the mountainous

Ski-jumping, anyone?

*Ruth's Diner,
Lake Placid, N.Y.*

terrain. Climbing lanes abound, so going slow for viewing or fast to get by the lookers is easy.

Lake Placid is a sophisticated town for the region,
with its Olympic training facilities, New York City summer residents, and international activities calendar. If
you've been on the road too long and need a little
culture, Lake Placid is a place to recharge your civilization batteries. The range of restaurants is wide, from
Ruth's Diner to after-theater dessert and late night
suppers. The ride out of town, up the hill to Saranac
Lake, is nice but a bit commercial.

The loop around Saranac Lake (Route 3 west to
Route 30 north to Route 186 east to Route 86 east) is fun.
Route 3 is long and straight with dips in the road.

Route 30 is especially challenging, with its 90- degree turns and twists providing excitement to contrast
with the scenic beauty. The degree of difficulty will be
determined by your speed. There are state parks (for
example, **Fish Creek Pond,** just out of Saranac on Route
30 north) that have swimming and other camping facilities on the lake for you to picnic, rest and/or savor your
experience. But not too long, because after Lake Placid,
Route 86 east narrows and climbs through **Wilmington
Notch** to the **Veterans Highway** to the top of Whiteface

Mountain (it's $4.00). The views are breathtaking! The Veterans Highway itself is a left where 86 east takes a right at a T in Wilmington, N.Y. If you are economizing, the atmospheric testing center just below the toll booth on Veterans Highway provides similar but lower views. Be nice, though, since it's not a public way.

The return to Route 86 east gives you a nice winding ride down from the high country into Jay, N.Y., where Route 9N follows the Ausable River directly (follow signs) to Route 9 and the famed **Ausable Chasm.** This is a natural phenomenon of waterfalls, deep gorges and a myriad of rock formations carved by eons of rushing water from the Ausable River. By the way, Ausable River means a river of sand in French. You can take a walking and boat tour.

The best find was **Harold's Bar.** Just follow the walkway out behind the tourist center, across the old

Once around the block: Lake Saranac

Ausable Chasm

bridge by the dam. Harold will provide a nonstop history since the thirties, a few times over, in the space of a cold drink. It's less expensive than the tourist center, the entertainment by Harold is free, and the horseshoe pits are beside the dam. Show him his picture in this book. He'll enjoy it every time!

The way back to Crown Point meanders alongside Lake Champlain on Route 22. The views of the lake and mountains will keep you company all the way home.

Two ferry crossings offer alternate modes and roads back to Crown Point. The first ferry, just down Route 373 east from Ausable Chasm, crosses from Port Kent to downtown Burlington. Then take Vermont Route 7 south to Route 22A south at Vergennes to Route 17 west. The second—and, I think, better if Burlington is not your destination—is the ferry from Essex, N.Y. to Charlotte, Vt.

Essex is a charming little town in which to eat. The **Old Dock Restaurant** is surrounded on three sides by water, just within view of the ferry. Don't bother to count the number of ferries you missed. The ferry, which runs every half hour, is a pretty 30-minute ride with the Adirondacks and the Green Mountains as a backdrop. It's inexpensive—$5.75 for two and a steed—and it provides a break from two-wheeled transportation (be sure to put the bike on the center stand and don't take it off until the ferry bumps the dock for the last time). When you disembark, grab Route 7 south to Route 22A south to Route 17 west back to Crown Point, N.Y.

The moose are gone but Harold's here

Essex Ferry, connecting Essex, N.Y. with Charlotte, Vt. across Lake Champlain

The Grand Isle Loop

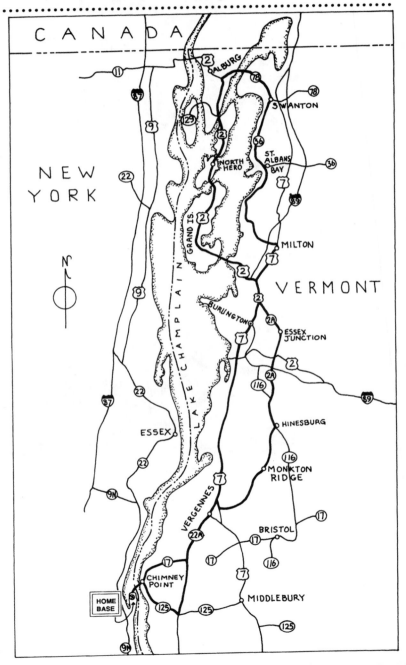

The Grand Isle Loop

....

Distance	*180 to 200 miles (288 to 320 kilometers)*
Speed	*Dirt to 60* MPH *(dirt to 100* KPH*)*
Highlights	*Scenic; water and mountains all the way*

The Route from Crown Point

→ Take right out of campground to Vermont Route 125 at the Champlain Bridge.

→ Route 125 to Route 22A north just above Bridport.

→ Route 22A north to Route 7 north at Vergennes.

→ Route 7 north to Route 2 west/Route 7 north at Winooski.

→ Route 2 west at Chimney Corner.

→ Route 2 west to Route 78 east at Alburg.

→ Route 78 east to Route 36 south at Swanton.

→ Route 36 south to Georgia Shore Road at St. Albans Bay (follow the lake).

→ Georgia Shore Road to Lake Road at West Milton.

→ Lake Road to Route 7 south at Checkerberry Village.

→ Route 7 south to Route 2A east above Colchester.

→ Route 2A east to Route 116 south just after St. George.

→ Route 116 south to Monkton Ridge Road at Hinesburg.

→ Monkton Ridge Road to Route 7 north at junction.

→ Route 7 north to Route 22A south at junction.

→ Route 22A south to Route 17 west at Addison.

→ Route 17 west to Crown Point, N.Y. (signs for bridge to New York).

Oldest log cabin in the United States, built by Jedediah Hyde, Jr. in 1783.

This loop is the most scenic of the three in the Lakes Journey. The biggest challenge here is to keep from getting into trouble while you gawk at Lake Champlain, the wildlife, and mountains. Routes 125 to 22A to 7 are two-lane highways for your morning wakeup. There are, of course, many places to chow down in Burlington, whether you are watching the sun set over the lake or rise over the Green Mountains.

The ride really starts unfolding on Route 2 west, crossing the causeway onto Grand Isle. The causeway allows for water views wherever you look. Of historical note is the **Hyde Log Cabin,** the oldest log cabin in the United States, located just north of the village of Grand Isle. Another place to stop is at the **Samuel de Champlain Statue,** sculpted at Canada's EXPO '67, off Route 129 on the Isle La Motte. The statue is also the site of **St. Anne's Shrine,** which holds daily services. There is very little else on Isle La Motte, adding to its secluded charm.

Return to Route 2 north via Route 129 and continue to Route 78 east, which cuts a swath through the wetlands of the Missisquoi National Wildlife Refuge as it follows the river of the same name. In Swanton pick up Route 36. This road never deviates more than 50 yards

*Statue of Samuel
de Champlain, on
Isle La Motte*

from the shores of Lake Champlain. On the lake side of
the road are summer cottages, with rolling fields ascending from the banks on the opposite side. This is a
rural setting with little traffic, so take your time and
don't hurt your neck stretching like the herons.

Just at the head of St. Albans Bay, about ten miles
south of Swanton on Route 36 heading south, you will
see signs for **Kill Kare State Park.** The right turn makes
you wonder where the road leads. DO IT! The park is at
the end of a small peninsula with picnic tables and BBQ
set-ups, and is a perfect escape from "NumButt." If you

In this modest building are the best French fries in Vermont.

are even more adventurous, the park service offers launch rides, people and gear only, to Burton Island and Wood's Island for camping.

Burton Island has all the modern camping conveniences, while Wood's Island is limited to five parties and a "carry out what you carry in" primitive wilderness setting.

Back out on Route 36 south, the road forks in a small village about a mile after the turnoff to Kill Kare. Bear right, leaving Route 36 for Georgia Shore Road. You will recognize the turn because Route 36 heads away from the lake, while the road of choice goes where you want to go: hugging the coast of Lake Champlain. There is a mile and a half stretch of hard, packed road bed about six miles south of St. Albans Bay, easy to negotiate with minimal dust envelopment. When the road forks again, bear left onto Lake Road to Route 7 south.

If you want to go into Burlington, stay on Route 7 south/Route 2 east until you reach Route 116 south. **Al's French Frys** is just before Route 116 on Route 2 if you are a fry meister.

If you want to circumnavigate Burlington, pick up Route 2A east off of Route 2. It will merge with Route

116 south of St. George. It is one of the better city bypasses.

Scooting back to Crown Point, N.Y., Route 116 will take a 90-degree left just below Hinesburg. When Route 116 takes the 90 degree turn go straight onto Monkton Ridge Road. These 15 miles of rolling farmland heaven, with some sweeping turns, are practically a direct shot into Vergennes. At the intersection of Monkton Ridge Road and Route 7, take Route 7 north. Less than a mile up Route 7, Route 22A intersects. Take Route 22A south into and out of Vergennes. Pick up Route 17 west at Addison for more of the countryside. This brings you to the Lake Champlain bridge and home again.

Places of Interest

NEW YORK

Ausable Chasm Harold's Bar, three-minute walk from behind Chasm entrance across the old bridge by the dam. Phone (518) 834-9907. Daily, noon 'til Harold decides to close. Harold is always there with a story behind Ausable Chasm. Horseshoes, cold drinks, picnic tables. $

Bolton Landing Jules' Diner, Route 9N. No Phone. Daily 6:00 a.m. to 7:00 p.m. Jules' motto: Good food, generous portions. $$

Crown Point Crown Point State Park, at Lake Champlain bridge, R.D. #1, Crown Point 12928. Phone (518) 597-3603. Open daily mid-April to mid-October. Grab the lean-to if you can.

Essex Old Dock Restaurant, Route 22. Phone (518) 963-4232. Daily lunch and dinner mid-May through mid-October. Center of town, casual, outdoor bar and grill. Reservations. $$$

Lake Placid Ruth's Diner, Main Street (Rte. 86). Phone (518) 523-3271. Daily 6:00 a.m. to 8:00 p.m. Lots of good food, good prices. $$

Saranac Lake Fish Creek Pond State Park, Route 30 north. Phone (518) 891-4560. All the amenities plus beach and lake swimming. Reservations accepted.

Pontiac Restaurant, 100 Main St. (opposite the Hotel Saranac). Phone (518) 891-5200. Sunday 10:00 a.m. to 5:00 p.m.; Monday 10:00 to 3:00 p.m; Tuesday to Thursday 10:30 a.m. to 9:00 p.m. Light foods and sandwiches; fresh, delicious food and the wait is worth it. $$

VERMONT

South Burlington Al's French Frys, 1251 Williston Road (Route 2). Phone (802) 862-9203. Daily 11:00 a.m. to 11:00 p.m. Superb French fries and all fried foods. $$

Grand Isle North Hero State Park, Route 2. Phone (802) 372-8727. Open May through mid-October. On Lake Champlain, the campground is excellent, well kept, available with firewood, BBQs, and beach.

Middlebury Woody's Restaurant, 5 Bakery Lane. Phone (802) 388-4182. Daily, 11:30 a.m. to midnight. Casual dining and drinking, outside decks, art deco interior, innovative menu. $$

Travel Information

· ·

NEW YORK

Road Conditions and Weather
Phone (800) 843-7623 in N.Y., (800) 247-7204 outside N.Y., Thruway emergencies (800) 842-2233.

Department of Economic Development
Albany 12245. Phone (800) 225-5697. I Love NY travel guides (by county), Outdoor Recreation publication, state parks and historic sites.

Warren County Tourism Office
Phone (800) 365-1050. I Love NY Camping and Accommodations; Guide for the Adirondacks.

VERMONT

Vermont Travel Division
134 State Street, Montpelier 05602. Phone (802) 828-3236. Official state guide and touring map, Vermont Vacation Guide, country inns, annual events calendar, traveler's guidebook.

Emergency and Medical Assistance

. . . .

NEW YORK

Glens Falls Glens Falls Hospital, 100 Park Street. Phone (518) 792-3151.

Lake Placid Adirondack Medical Center, Church Street. (518) 523-3311.

Saranac Lake Adirondack Medical Center, Lake Colby Drive. (518) 891-4141.

VERMONT

Berlin Central Vermont Hospital, Fisher Road (Exit 7, Interstate 89). Phone (802) 229-9121.

Burlington Medical Center Hospital of Vermont, Colchester Avenue. Phone (802) 656-2434.

Middlebury Porter Medical Center, South Street. Phone (802) 388-7901.

Randolph Gifford Memorial Hospital, 44 S. Main Street. Phone (802) 728-4441.

St. Albans Northwestern Medical Center, Fairfield Street, between the Interstate and Main Street. Phone (802) 524-5911.

St. Johnsbury Northeastern Regional Hospital, Hospital Drive. Phone (802) 748-8141.

Cruisin' The Berkshires

The Berkshires are a range of low mountains located for the most part in western Massachusetts. Their borders extend north to Vermont, west to New York State, south to Connecticut and east to Massachusetts' Pioneer Valley. The rides set out here are designed to avoid traffic congestion and introduce you to the wide expanse of rolling hills, rivers, and lakes, while swinging by some of the more interesting sights in the region.

In summer, the region hosts a vast assortment of entertainment: theater and art at the Clark Museum in Williamstown, dance at Jacob's Pillow in Becket, the Norman Rockwell museum in Stockbridge, and good old rock n' roll at Woody's in Washington. Spring and fall are less populated; during those seasons you'll find less congested roads and off-season rates for everything, except during the first two weeks of October, when fall colors bring people from all over the country to view nature's spectacle.

For this journey, I created my base camp at the October Mountain State Forest, in Lee, near Lenox, Mass. Lenox is centrally located with a variety of places to stay, ranging from posh well-known inns to motels and campgrounds.

The best way to get to the Berkshires from Boston is the Mohawk Trail, (Mass. Route 2).

About 140 miles in length from Boston to the Berkshires, Route 2 starts as a four-lane highway near Boston and, west of Orange, Mass., narrows to two-lane twisties, scenic views and overlooks, and one hairpin turn.

From New York, grab U.S. Highway 684 north to the intersection of N.Y. Route 22 north. Hang a right at Haviland, N.Y. to Conn. Route 37 north to Conn. Route 7 north. This route is direct, with sufficient back road content to keep your interest, and picks up the Southern Berkshire loop. You may want to go home that way.

Biker's delight

On a clear day . . . (the Mohawk Trail)

The Northern Berkshire Loop

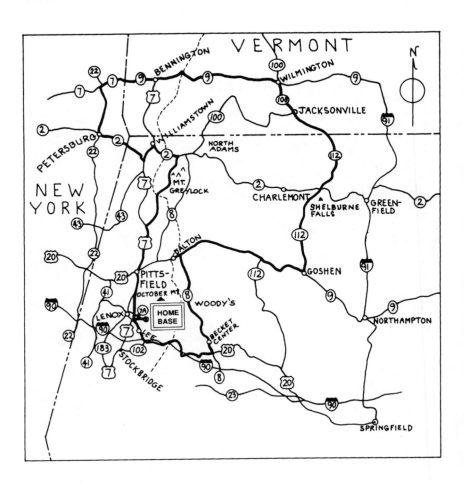

The Northern Berkshire Loop

Distance   *200 miles (333 kilometers)*

Speed   *20 to 60* MPH *(17 to 92* KPH*)*

Highlights   *Mountain climbs, river runs, rolling farmland*

The Route from Lenox, Mass.

→ Route 7A south to Route 7 south.

→ Route 7 south to Route 20 east.

→ Mass. Route 20 east to Route 8 north at Becket Center, Mass.

→ Route 8 north to Route 9 east, just east of Dalton.

→ Route 9 east to Route 112 north at Goshen.

→ Route 112 north into Vermont, then Vt. Route 100 north at Jacksonville, Vt.

→ Route 100 north to Route 9 west at Wilmington.

→ Route 9 west (it turns into N.Y. 7) to N.Y. Route 22 south, just west of Hoosick, N.Y.

→ Route 22 south to Route 2 east (Taconic Trail) at Petersburg.

→ Route 2 east into Massachusetts, to Mass. Route 7 north.

→ Route 7 north to Route 2 east at Williamstown.

→ Route 2 east to Notch Road before North Adams. Signs say TO GREYLOCK RESERVATION/STATE PARK.

→ Notch Road over Mt. Greylock to Rockwell Road.

→ Rockwell Road to Route 7 south.

→ Route 7 south to Route 7A south at Lenox.

The beginning of this loop is twisty along Route 20. Route 8, a narrow two-lane highway with lots of turns, follows the west branch of the Westfield River. If you aren't awake by now, these roads will wake you up.

North Adams

About 12 miles north of the intersection of Route 20 and Route 8 is **Woody's,** "the original rock n' roll palace," a funky roadhouse.

Just across the road from Woody's is Frost Road. Take it up about a mile to the intersection of Frost Road and Washington Mountain Road, take a left, and you're only 50 yards from **Bucksteep Manor,** an inn with campground, rustic cabins and live music at the bar located in the barn. If you make the Manor home base,

Babababaad to the bone

Bucksteep Manor

you can walk home after the dance—the only way if you are under the influence!

Upon leaving Bucksteep Manor, take a right on Washington Mountain Road and travel along the ridge into Pittsfield, crossing the Appalachian Trail.

Staying on Route 8 north, you travel the east side of the Berkshire Hills. Route 9 is a major two-lane highway. The fill-in material for the cracks in the asphalt caused me to slip on a hot summer day, even though I have a "sticky" Metzeler Marathon skin on the rear. Nothing dangerous, but a weird feeling. If you get scenery gawkers on Mass. Route 9, relax and enjoy the scenery with them.

Route 112 starts off as a well-maintained but Melba Toast type road, but only for a few miles. The farther north you go, the more narrow and winding it gets. Just before the junction of Route 2 and Route 112, you reach the towns of **Shelburne Falls** and **Buckland.**

I don't know where one town ends and the other begins, but it is worth stopping for food, a cool drink, and the **Bridge of Flowers,** an abandoned railroad trestle the townspeople beautified with plantings. Their effort shows in colors and scents.

Community spirit abounds at the Bridge of Flowers

There are three places to eat in Buckland, just across the bridge: **Marty's, Buckland Grille,** and **McCusker's.** The latter is an extensive specialty and natural food market. These are pretty much the last places to eat until you reach Wilmington, Vt., so either stock up or chow down.

Route 112 parallels the North River after you cross Route 2 headed for Vermont. You can tell when you've reached Vermont by the terrain. The land changes into hilly farm country and traffic drops off to almost nothing. There are two metal-decked bridges on Route 112, so keep a steady speed and do not hit the brakes.

Mass. Route 112 turns into Vt. Route 112, which intersects with Vt. Route 100. Route 100 is rural farmland all the way to Wilmington. As you pass through the center of Wilmington on Route 9, stop at **Dot's Restaurant** for breakfast or goooood four-alarm chili (five alarms being the max). The chef has won a couple of Vermont state ribbons for the chili.

After Wilmington, Route 9 is an easy, smooth, well-paved road that traverses the southern portion of the Green Mountain range. Panoramic vistas and lower gear riding await you on the west side of the mountain range as you enter New York State.

A three-state view

Route 22 is a straight two-lane highway that gets you from Hoosick to the Taconic Trail. The New York side of Route 2, an eight-mile hill climb, has a few frost heaves. The Massachusetts side, though, is beautiful enough to ride a couple of times. As you head north toward Williamstown, Mass., Route 7 is a two-lane highway which has vista views and some curves (see Central Berkshire Loop for discussion of Williamstown itself). About two miles east on Route 2 is Notch Road, the entrance road (small sign says STATE RESERVATION) to the **Mount Greylock State Reservation.**

Mt. Greylock, at 3,491 feet, is the highest peak in Massachusetts. The road winds up the north side of the mountain with switchbacks and hairpins, all unmarked. Climbing Mt. Greylock, with growing excitement at this new-found road, I was abruptly introduced to a foot-wide by six-inch-deep trench. The spinal compression made me an inch shorter than I was at the start of my journey. Soon after my trench warfare experience, a park ranger coming down the mountain in an old pickup truck flashed his lights and signaled me to stop. He leaned out his window and said "There are about three or four open trenches up ahead so be careful. They were supposed to pave them last week, but . . ." I thanked him and told him to be careful, since one of those animal trenches was ahead of him! There were five trenches cutting across the summit road, all unmarked.

As I got closer to the summit, I saw a small needle-like object on the summit to the west. This obelisk is a war memorial to Massachusetts' sons and daughters. It is remarkable, with a glass globe on the top standing guard over a three-state view.

The ride down the southwest face of Mt. Greylock was a second gear endeavor via a narrow road cut through a pine forest. You rejoin Route 7 south just above Lanesborough.

The farther south you go on Route 7, the straighter and more commercial the road gets. Once you pass through the town of Pittsfield, on the east side of Route 7 at the Pittsfield line, it's a short run into the village of Lenox.

Dakota, on the east side of Route 7 at the Pittsfield line, is a brass, fern, and oak restaurant with an audience ranging from suits to sweats. It offers the largest selection of salad bar materials and toppings I've ever seen.

Decisions, decisions

The Southern Berkshire Loop

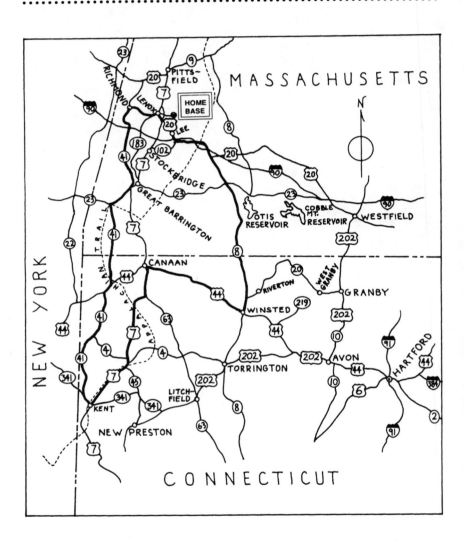

The Southern Berkshire Loop

Distance *180 to 200 miles (300 to 333 kilometers)*

Speed *20 to 55 MPH (33 to 92 KPH)*

Highlights *Rolling hills, vistas, river roads*

The Route from Lenox, Mass.

→ Route 7A south to Route 7 south.

→ Route 7 south to Route 20 east.

→ Route 20 east to Route 8 south at West Becket.

→ Route 8 south to Conn. Route 44 west at Winsted, Conn.

→ Route 44 west to Route 7 south just after East Canaan.

→ Route 7 south to Route 341 west at Kent. *

→ Route 341 west to Route 41 north (approx. 2.5 miles)

→ Mass. Route 41 north to Lenox Road in Richmond. (It is easier to pick up signs for Lenox).

→ Lenox Road merges with Richmond Road.

→ Richmond Road merges with Route 183 north.

→ Route 183 north to 7A at Lenox.

* Route Extension

Side trip or extension to loop for Hopkins Vineyards in New Preston, Conn.

→ Route 7 south to Route 45 south (just after Cornwall Bridge, follow signs for VINEYARDS).

→ Return via route 45 north to Route 341 west and resume loop.

This is a simpler route dedicated to a ride with grand vistas and views of the rolling countryside. Route 20 is busy until you get through East Lee. Up Route 20 past West Becket, on the north side of the road, is **Jacob's Pillow,** one of the foremost dance theaters in the region. The tickets are tough to get, so order ahead.

*The Colebrook
Reservoir . . . dam!*

Route 8 south offers a goodly number of twisties and follows the Farmington River about as close as you can without getting wet. As Route 8 broadens, it passes through 50- to 75-foot road cuts. The large body of water created by a dam on your left is the **Colebrook Reservoir.**

Pull into the work area and drive right onto the dam—the view is worth it!

A quick side trip or stopping area is the Granville State Forest in Connecticut and the nearby town of Riverton. The **Hitchcock Museum,** 200 yards off of Route 20 on River Road in Riverton, has an extensive collection of rare 19th century Hitchcock furniture.

Retrace your path back to Route 20 east and continue to Route 219 south (just before West Granby), then catch Route 44 west in New Hartford. Otherwise you'll get sucked into the vortex of Hartford, Conn.

Route 7 is a rural road with good surfaces and some turns. The road bisects a few towns that are small but can provide some "NumButt" breaks.

If you have the time and inclination, the side trip to **Hopkins Vineyards** is worth it. The inn and restaurant high on a hillside reminded me of a little Alpine village from my European travels. The wine is pretty good too.

Aim for the swill bucket, not the gullet at the tasting bar! If you swallow the wine, make it your last stop of the day.

Route 41 is made for a bike. One of my favorite reminders of the difference between bikers and "everybody else" came from the gas attendant at the intersection of Routes 7 and 341. When I asked him what Route 41 was like, he replied, "Where ya goin'?" When I replied "Lenox, Mass." he screwed up his face and scratched his head in one of those . . . looks asking, "Hell, why do you want to go 41? It's 15 miles outtayaway!" I thanked him and proceeded to have one decidedly delightful outtayaway trip!

Route 41 meanders north through Connecticut farms and villages, some with fully restored Victorian houses, others a little more tumbledown. Route 41 takes you all the way to Richmond, Mass., in a leisurely trip combining beauty with the goal of getting from nowhere to nowhere. The route gets more difficult to follow from Richmond, so follow the signs to Lenox. This is easier than looking for Lenox Road and its eventual merge with Route 183. The road is a little rough in spots, but worth the ride to come over the crest of a hill and overlook the Stockbridge Bowl.

Hopkins Inn

The Central Berkshire Loop

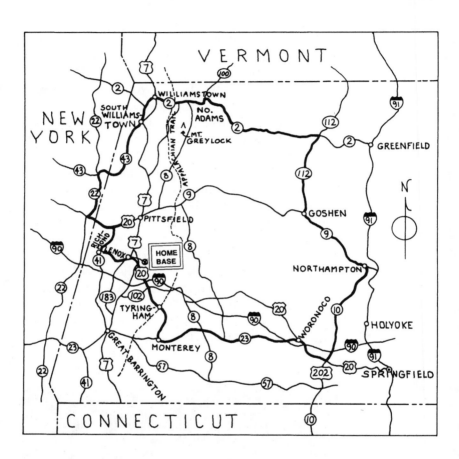

The Central Berkshire Loop

Distance *160 miles (267 kilometers)*

Speed *20 to 55* MPH *(33 to 92* KPH)

Highlights *Rural roads, scenic views, unusual museums and galleries*

The Route from Lenox, Mass.

→ Route 183 south, bear right onto Richmond Road at the Tanglewood Music Center.

→ Richmond Road merges into Lenox Road, to Route 41 north at Richmond.

→ Route 41 north to Route 20 west at Hancock Shaker Village.

→ Route 20 west to N.Y. Route 22 north at New Lebanon, New York.

→ Route 22 north to Route 43 north at Hancock.

→ Route 43 north to Mass. Route 7 north at South Williamstown, Mass.

→ Route 7 north to Route 2 east at Williamstown.

→ Route 2 east to Route 112 south at Shelburne Falls.

→ Route 112 south to Route 9 east at Goshen.

→ Route 9 east to Route 10 south at Northampton.

→ Route 10 south to Route 20 west at Westfield.*

→ Route 20 west to Route 23 west at Woronoco.

→ Route 23 west to center of Monterey.

→ Turn right onto Tyringham Road (follow signs for Tyringham).

→ Bear right at T at the end of Tyringham Road (sign says EAST LEE).

→ Tyringham Road merges with Route 102.

→ Route 102 north to Route 20 west at East Lee (Katy's Diner & Dan's Diesel).

→ Route 20 west to Route 183 at Lenox.

* Route Extension to NBA Hall of Fame

→ Route 20 east at Westfield to Route 5 south at Springfield.

→ Take Memorial exit (next OFF ramp) to rotary.

→ Go halfway around the rotary and over Memorial Bridge.

→ First right after Memorial Bridge onto Columbus Avenue.

→ N.B.A. is on right.

* Route Extension to Indian Motorcycle Museum

→ Route 20 east to Interstate 91 south in Springfield.

→ Interstate 91 south to Interstate 291 east at junction.

→ Interstate 291 east to Exit 4, St. James Avenue.

→ Bear right off the exit ramp onto Page Boulevard.

→ Follow sign to the museum; it is a few hundred yards on Hendee St.

From the center of Lenox, on Route 183 heading toward Richmond, bear right at the **Tanglewood Music Center.** Tanglewood is the summer home of the Boston Symphony Orchestra. During the summer schedule you can sit on the lawn or buy seats for the performances. The park is lovely; bring a picnic, whether the orchestra is performing or not.

Richmond Road is a twisty and bumpy hill climb. Why do curves and bumps always go hand and hand? After cresting the hill, Richmond Road merges with Lenox Road, which offers more curves and little traffic, scenic farm country, and lots of rolling ups and downs. Pick up Route 41 north.

At the intersection of Routes 41 and 20 is the **Hancock Shaker Village,** a restored settlement with 20 buildings on 1000 acres, illustrating the Shaker lifestyle.

From here it's a quick hop to N.Y. Routes 22 and 43 north, an easy highway drive. Route 43 north, which follows the Green River, is well constructed and has few challenges before intersecting with Mass. Route 7 in South Williamstown.

Be it ever so humble. The Sterling and Francine Clark Art Institute.

Williamstown is a Berkshire town with a blend of highbrow culture and college environment. The **Williamstown Theater Festival** features name stars at reasonable prices. Reservations are a must.

Stop at the **Sterling and Francine Clark Art Institute,** which houses the largest permanent collection of Renoirs in the United States. In addition to many works of the Old Masters and French Impressionists, the museum has an outstanding collection depicting the Old West through sculpture and paintings by Winslow Homer and Frederic Remington.

The story behind the Clark collection and museum is one of sibling rivalry. It seems the boys, Stephen and Robert Sterling, heirs to the Singer sewing machine fortune (granddaddy Clark was Isaac Singer's business partner and was founder of Coats & Clark Thread Company), played a game of one-upsmanship. In the end, Stephen donated his collection to the National Museum in Washington, D.C. Not to be outdone, Robert Sterling and his bride, Francine, built their own home to house their treasures which they in turn transformed into the impressive museum—or mausoleum—bearing their name.

After all that culture you can get set for a little Americana. North of Williamstown on Route 7 is the **Chef's Hat.** The Farmer Jones special breakfast of pancakes, eggs, and all the fixin's, interacts with you to lower the center of gravity on your bike by an inch.

The Mohawk Trail, Route 2, was once a footpath used by the Indians of Five Nations. The Pocumtuck Indians, as the legend goes, blazed this trail across the mountains from Deerfield, Mass., to Troy, N.Y., in order to invade the land of the Mohawks. The Dutch settlers in Albany negotiated a peace treaty to end the Indian

History and heritage

war, but on the way to ratify the treaty, Saheda, a Mohawk prince, was murdered on the trail. In retaliation, the Mohawks killed the entire Pocumtuck tribe in one day.

Now the Trail winds through a couple of towns until you pass North Adams, round a hairpin turn and start to climb the Hoosac Range. As previously mentioned, this is a great stretch of asphalt. If you want to extend the loop try Route 100 north to Briggsville and into Vermont, then back by Route 112 south. This is a twisty rural ride which adds about 20 miles to the Route 2 (Mohawk Trail) leg of the loop.

Route 9 is a wide two-lane highway, almost always under repair, but the sections under construction are well marked. Route 10 south out of Northampton down to Route 20 is a bit commercial in places, but is a direct way to Route 20. At Route 20 you have the choice of going east into Springfield and the **Indian Motorcycle Museum** and **National Basketball Association Hall of Fame** or taking Route 20 west to Route 23.

Route 23 is a special road: smooth, twisty turns, scenic hills, and deep pine forest are along the entire road. It runs straight into the Catskill Mountains and is a great way to enter or leave the Berkshires on their western side.

Monterey, on Route 23, is 25 miles west from Route 20. In the center of town, take a right onto Tyringham Road to what the locals affectionately call **The Gingerbread House**, a.k.a. the Tyringham Art Galleries, one of the most unusual structures in the region.

The building, which looks like the witch's house in the fairy tale of Hansel and Gretel, was built as a design studio by the late Sir Henry Kitson (Sir Henry, the artist who sculpted the famous Minuteman Statue in Lexington, Mass., is represented in the National Gallery in Washington, D.C.). The roof of the Gingerbread House is made of shingles layered to simulate a thatched roof and carved to represent the contour of the Berkshires in the fall. You can see the texture sculpted to give the

Who's knocking on my front door? "Gingerbread house" in Tyringham, Mass.

appearance of rolling hills and the burnished coloring of fall. The art gallery inside contains unique indoor and outdoor sculptures, mobiles, and ceramics.

Tyringham Road intersects with Route 102 and Route 20 just across from Katy's Kitchen and Dan's Diesel Stop. Take Route 20 west, which brings you back to Lee. In Lee, stop at **Joe's Diner,** which serves a 25-cent cup of Joe and a slice of 1950s Americana until midnight. Joe had run the diner 24 hours a day until 1991. Look at the pictures of famous patrons adorning the wall. How many can you name without peeking at the autographs? One of the waitresses rides a Norton and another a Softail, so you can expect empathy and good stories to be served with the food.

Places of Interest

· ·

CONNECTICUT

New Preston   Hopkins Vineyards and Inn, Hopkins Road. Phone, Inn: (203) 868-7295. Vineyard: (203) 868-7954. Open April to November. Dining year-round except for Mondays. Quaint inn plus dining room. Terrace dining in summer, serving Austrian and Swiss fare, reflecting the Alpine image of local scenery. Reservations for the inn are a must. $$$

MASSACHUSETTS

Lanesborough   Bascom Lodge, Summit of Mt. Greylock. Phone (413) 743-1591. One sitting, family style, 6:00 p.m. 100-mile views from the top. Reservations for dinner by noon. $$

Mount Greylock State Reservation, Rockwell Road. Phone (413) 499-4262. Thirty-five sites, primitive, highest point in Massachusetts. On the Appalachian Trail, picnics.

Lee   Joe's Diner, Route 20 and Main Street. Phone (413) 243-9756. Open daily 6:00 a.m. to midnight. Famous 1950s luncheonette, good food, cheap daily specials. $

October Mountain State Forest, Woodland Road. Phone (413) 243-1778. Fifty sites, well kept, close to loops and town. My base camp for the journey. Hot showers and campfires.

Lenox   Cherry's, 6 Franklin Street. No phone. Open daily 6:30 a.m. to 8:00 p.m. (Monday and Tuesday to 2:00 p.m.). Managed by local school kids, open mike Friday 'til midnight, daily specials for lunch and dinner. $

Pittsfield   Dakota, Route 7. Phone (413) 499-7900. Daily lunch and dinner. Fresh continental fare. Largest salad bar I know. Treat yourself. $$$

Shelburne Falls   Marty's Riverside Cafe, 4 State Street. Phone (413) 625-2570. Open year-round, 11:00 a.m. to 9:00 p.m., closed Mondays. Funky natural food on the river, specials daily. $$

Springfield   Indian Motorcycle Museum, 33 Hendee Street. Phone (413) 737-2624. Open March to November, 10:00 a.m. to 5:00 p.m., and December to February, 1:00 to 5:00 p.m. Admission $3.00. It's a pilgrimage!

National Basketball Hall of Fame, 1150 West Columbus Avenue. Phone (413) 781-6500. Open year-round 9:00 a.m. to 5:00 p.m., July and August until 6:00 p.m. Admission $6.00. If you are a fan, this is a behind-the-back slam dunk.

Washington   Bucksteep Manor, Washington Mountain Road. Phone (413) 623-5535. Campground, inn, cabins, and rock 'n roll barn. $$

Woody's, Route 8. Phone (413) 623-8302. Open 7:00 p.m. to ???, mid-June to Labor Day. The original rock 'n roll palace. The graffiti in the women's room is badder than the men's! $

Williamstown   Sterling and Francine Clark Art Museum, 225 South Street. Phone (413) 458-9545. Open year-round, Tuesday to Sunday 10:00 a.m. to 5:00 p.m. Culture and art, free of charge.

VERMONT

Wilmington   Dot's Restaurant, Route 9. Phone (802) 464-7284. Open daily 5:30 a.m. to 3:00 p.m. Diner and luncheonette. Cajun omelets, four-star chili, homemade muffins. $

Travel Information

CONNECTICUT

Department of Economic Development, Tourism Division

865 Brook Street, Rocky Hill 06067. Phone (800) CT BOUND. Maps, brochures, campgrounds and state parks.

MASSACHUSETTS

Berkshire State Forest Guide

Phone (413) 442-8928. Everything you want to know.

Berkshire Hills Conference Visitors Bureau

Berkshire Common, South Street, Pittsfield. Phone (413) 443-9186. Museums of Massachusetts, B & B Guide, guide to the wilderness trails, guide to Massachusetts campgrounds.

Spirit of Massachusetts, Office of Tourism

100 Cambridge Street, Boston 02202. Phone (800) 447-6277. Guide by region, bed and bath directory, maps, and state parks, forests and campgrounds.

NEW YORK

Dept. of Economic Development

Albany 12245. Phone (800) 225-5697. "I love NY" Travel Guides (by county), outdoor recreation publication, State Parks and Historic Sites.

VERMONT

Vermont Travel Division

134 State Street, Montpelier. Phone (802) 828-3236. Official State Guide and Touring Map, Vermont Vacation Guide, Country Inns, Annual Events Calendar, Traveler's Guidebook.

Emergency and Medical Assistance

MASSACHUSETTS

Great Barrington Fairview Hospital, 29 Lewis Avenue. Phone (413) 528-0790.

Lee Massachusetts State Police Barracks. Phone (413) 243-0670.

North Adams North Adams Regional Hospital, Hospital Avenue. Phone (413) 663-3701.

Pittsfield Berkshire Medical Center, 725 North Street. Phone (413) 447-2000.

The Southern Coast

The southern coast of New England—Connecticut, Rhode Island, and Massachusetts—was the whaling and fishing capital of the United States in the mid-1800s. Even today, New Bedford, Massachusetts is home to the largest fishing fleet in the country, more than 300 ships. If you want some idea of why the ocean is so important here, consider this: although Rhode Island, the smallest state in the U.S., is only 45 miles across, it has more than 400 miles of shoreline.

It is because of this geography that the loops on this journey are short and the views from the steed are to the horizon. This journey is scenic, historic, and a real "beach." I integrated interior roads into the journey for variety in scenery and ride mix.

Home base for this "SeaFairing" journey is **Burlingame State Park** on Cookestown Road, off Route 1, between Westerly and Charlestown, Rhode Island. Fisherman's Memorial State Park (reservations required) is an alternative off Route 108 between Narragansett and Point Judith, R.I.

The Bay Loop crosses the border between Rhode Island and Massachusetts a number of times, and the Inland Loop comes close to crossing the Massachusetts border from Connecticut. A word of CAUTION: As of this writing there is no helmet law in Rhode Island or Connecticut, but Massachusetts enforces the requirement strictly.

The Bay Loop

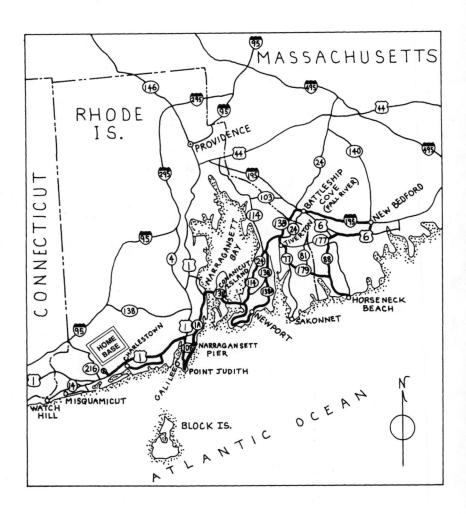

The Bay Loop

· ·

Distance *160 to 210 miles (266 to 350 kilometers)*

Speed *10 to 60* MPH *(17 to 100* KPH*)*

Highlights *Lots of history, coastlines, and museums*

The Route from Burlingame State Park

→ R.I. Route 1 north to Route 108 south at exit.

→ Route 108 south to Point Judith, R.I. Turn around.

→ Route 108 north to Ocean Avenue, Narragansett.

→ Ocean Avenue merges with Route 1A north at Narragansett Pier.

→ Route 1A north to Route 138 east at intersection.

→ Route 138 east to first exit after Newport Bridge at SCENIC NEWPORT sign. Continue to follow Newport signs.

→ Bear right onto Thames Street when the sign for Memorial Boulevard and Route 138 indicates a left.

→ Thames Street to Ocean Drive.

→ Ocean Drive to Bellevue Avenue.

→ Bellevue Avenue to Memorial Boulevard.

→ Memorial Boulevard to Route 138A north at Middletown.

→ Route 138A north merges with Route 138 north.

→ Route 138 north to Route 24 north.

→ Route 24 north to Route 138 north at Tiverton.

→ Route 138 north into Massachusetts.

→ Mass. Route 138 north to Interstate 195 east at Fall River.

→ Interstate 195 east to exit 15 (DOWNTOWN NEW BEDFORD); follow the WHALE sign to the Whaling Museum.

→ From Whaling Museum follow signs to I-195 west; get on Route 6 west at New Bedford.

→ Route 6 west to Route 177 west.

→ Route 177 west to Route 88 south at junction.

→ Route 88 south to Horseneck Beach.

→ Return Route 88 north to Route 179 west at junction.

→ Route 179 west to Route 77 north at junction.

→ Route 77 north to Route 24 south at Tiverton.

→ Route 24 south to Route 114 south at end.

→ Route 114 south to Route 138 west, above Newport.

→ Route 138 west to Route 1A south at junction.

→ Route 1A south to Route 1 south at Narragansett.

→ Route 1 south to Matunuck Beach Road.

→ Matunuck Beach Rd. to Matunuck School Rd.

→ Matunuck School Road merges with Route 1 just past Charlestown.

→ Route 1 to home base.

The Bay Loop can easily take two to three days depending on how much beach, culture, and sight-seeing you want to do. This is an extensive trip, although the mileage is short. The Bay Loop passes some of the most beautiful beaches and breathtaking shoreline in New England. Some of the oldest shipping ports in the nation are along the way.

From the late 1800s to the mid 1900s, some of the wealthiest people in the world chose Newport and its surroundings to live in. Narragansett Bay is still the summer playground for the rich, but more modest folk can play here, too.

The first things I noticed while riding on Route 1 east/north from home base (the highway department is inconsistent in their signage) are the exit signs on the way to Narragansett. Every one of the signs names a beach: Charlestown Beach Road, Moonstruck Beach Road, Matunuck Beach Road, and just for variety, a sign for the Theater by the Sea. All within ten miles of where I first got on the road.

Route 108 south, off of Route 1, is a four-lane undivided highway. If you decide to go to Block Island, take Galilee Road just after **Fisherman's Memorial State Park.** This takes you into Galilee, where the Block Island Ferry docks.

Point Judith Light

Back in 1902, Tom Mann, a fisherman from Nova Scotia who settled here, felt the village resembled its namesake from biblical times. One day an old timer repairing his net was asked by a stranger where he was. The old man replied, "Galilee." "And what is that?" the stranger said, pointing to the other side of the breachway. The old timer thought for a minute and said, "Well, if this is Galilee, then that's Jerusalem." No, you can't get from Rhode Island's Galilee to Jerusalem by water.

Continuing south on Route 108 you arrive at Point Judith Light. The last German U-Boat sunk in World War II was two miles off the point.

Ocean Road is your first right returning on Route 108. Over the next eight miles, you'll pass eight beaches. **Scarborough State Beach** is a surfing beach, so there's plenty of action at the sea and on the shore for us boys and girls who are young or young at heart.

Farther up the road is the town of Narragansett and its even more active beaches, with free surfing lessons available on Wednesdays at noon. The surfing report is on 95.5 FM at 8:20 a.m. Fridays and Saturdays, for you radio-equipped travelers. For 24-hour surf conditions, call (401) 789-1954. The best features of Narragansett

Coast Guard
Restaurant on
Ocean Road

town beach are the so-close-at-hand establishments serving cold refreshments. The **Coast Guard Restaurant** has a nice observation deck for the scenery.

Narragansett was (and is) an elegant summer resort. In the late 1800's rich Newporters would ferry across the Bay to partake of the entertainment offered by the Narragansett Casino, a country club by today's definition. A fire destroyed the casino in 1900. All that is left is the arch over Ocean Road.

Route 1A north intersects with Route 138 about ten miles up. Follow signs east to Newport and Jamestown Bridge. The Jamestown Bridge and the Newport Bridge on the other side of Conanicut Island offer spectacular views of Narragansett Bay. The Jamestown Bridge (CAUTION: the top portion of the bridge is metal decking) deposits you onto Conanicut Island, as serene as its more famous neighbor, Newport, is sophisticated. If you stay straight on East Shore Road, rather than following Route 138, you arrive in the village of Jamestown. Park in the lot at the harbor and have a cup of award winning coffee and pastry at **East Ferry Market & Deli** out on the patio overlooking the Bay.

Facing the water from your patio perch, take the road in front of you to the right, following the shoreline to **Fort Wetherill State Park,** once a shore artillery battery. Picnic tables and the usual day tripper facilities are available from Memorial Day to Labor Day. The park itself remains open all year. This is a favorite spot among scuba divers.

I took the access road to the end of the park and came upon an imposing open chain link fence and sign reading GOVERNMENT PROPERTY - NO TRESPASSING. Naturally, it aroused my curiosity. Driving into the yard, I could see half-buried structures that were artillery bunkers for the fort. A little dirt road that climbed up between the bunkers brought me to the top of Narragansett Bay, overlooking Newport and its mansions.

Exiting the park, take your first paved left, Hamilton Street. At the next intersection go straight ahead; a small town beach will be on your left. Go across the isthmus. On the right, just at the end of the isthmus, is the entrance to **Fort Getty State Park,** a seaside campground sitting on a small knoll, with a magnificent view, overlooking the mouth of Narragansett Bay. Although it is usually full during camping season, it's worth a drive through.

Narragansett
Casino Arch

Beavertail
Lighthouse

Bear left onto Beaver Tail Road just after the Fort Getty entrance to get to **Beavertail Lighthouse State Park.** The lighthouse is the third oldest in the country, built in 1749 after the Boston Light (1716) and the Brant Point Light on Nantucket (1746). The museum inside commemorates the lighthouses of Rhode Island and their keepers.

Retrace your route back to Route 138 east and cross the Newport Bridge from Jamestown to Newport. Keep one eye on the bridge, but check out the harbor and the yachts. Welcome to the land of the rich and the tourists! You have to put up with the traffic in the town of Newport (keep right on the main drag and bear right when the road splits down Thames Street) to get to the **Ten Mile Drive.** Take a right onto Wellington Avenue as you circumnavigate the harbor.

The Ten Mile Drive is a scenic ride along the coast past all the humble abodes of the more fortunate. Two outstanding examples are **The Hammersmith Farm** and **The Inn at Castle Hill.**

The Hammersmith Farm, a.k.a. "The Summer White House," was Jackie Kennedy Onassis' mother's (Mrs. Hugh Auchincloss) summer home. Jackie had her debut and her wedding reception with JFK here. The

Hammersmith Farm, JFK's summer White House

fifty acres of farmland by the sea make up the only working farm in Newport. Scenes from "The Great Gatsby," with Robert Redford, were filmed here.

The Inn at Castle Hill just down the road (watch for signs since you can't see it from the road) offers a panoramic view of the Bay. Watch the great ships entering and leaving the harbor while you sit on the patio enjoying something cold to drink, then walk to the cliff's edge to see Castle Hill Light.

Back on the Ten Mile Drive, you will shadow the ocean's edge until you reach Bellevue Avenue. This is where the Great Mansions of Newport were (Vander)built. You can tour them (it takes a good day to do all eight properties). If you are just passing by, drive into each of the boulevards (I hesitate to call them driveways) and get a feel for the grandeur of these elegant summer homes. Imagine your arrival as a guest, then play it out: at the **Astor's Beechwood Mansion,** the Beechwood Theatrical Group welcomes your arrival as if you were one of the original "Newport 400" arriving for the season in the 1890s.

Once your "coming out" party is over, rejoin Memorial Boulevard, merge with Route 138 north, pass through Tiverton, R.I., and head straight for Fall River,

Mass. Just after the Rhode Island border, on Route 138 in Massachusetts, is the bright orange, un-miss-able **George's Root Beer.** George makes his own root beer, and it is delicious.

Follow the signs to **Battleship Cove** and **Fall River Heritage State Park.** Park there and walk around the cove to the ships. The USS Massachusetts, affectionately called "Big Mamie," by her crew, is over 200 yards long. You can tour the entire ship, climb inside the turrets, and aim the anti-aircraft guns on the main deck. You can also patrol a PT boat, a destroyer, and a submarine.

The Marine Museum down the street has a excellent exhibition focused on the Titanic, including a video of her rediscovery and a 28-foot replica. To get a little physical, just to the left of the Museum is **Inside the Park, Inc.,** where you can "hit a few" in batting cages on the second floor of the warehouse with pitching from 45 to 85 MPH, hardball or softball.

Exiting Heritage State Park, follow signs to Interstate Route 195 and go east to Exit 15, DOWNTOWN NEW BEDFORD. Follow the whale (picture) signs to the front of the **Whaling Museum.**

From the water's edge (The Inn at Castle Hill)

CAUTION: New Bedford still has cobblestone streets in the Historic District, which does nothing for traction, especially if wet.

The New Bedford Whaling Museum is devoted to American whaling, with a multi-media approach to this period in history. There are paintings, artifacts, harpoons, whale skeletons, and murals, and an 85-foot exact half scale model built in 1916, of the whaling ship Lagoda. You can shiver your own timbers on board—it's as if you climbed into one of those "ship in the bottle" models!

The theater shows a 22-minute film of a whaling expedition, filmed in 1922 in New Bedford on board an actual whaling ship. The actor portrays Charles W. Morgan, the boat's owner and namesake of the Charles W. Morgan Whaleship moored in Mystic Seaport, Conn., and built in New Bedford.

Across the street is the **Seamen's Bethel.** Built in 1832, it provided inspiration for Herman Melville's whaling classic, *Moby Dick*. Melville's sister, whom he came to visit often, lived in New Bedford. The cenotaphs (memorial stones on the walls) commemorate sailors who sailed out of New Bedford and never returned. The small church was remodeled after a fire in

Bringing in the
BIG GUNS

The Marine Museum at Fall River

1866, reversing the original seating. Herman Melville's pew before the remodeling sat next to the Wm. Swain centograph. Mr. Swain died at sea in similar circumstances to Captain Ahab's in *Moby Dick*. Chapters seven and eight of *Moby Dick* speak about the Seamen's Bethel and the Bowsprit Pulpit. The plaque at the entrance reads from the novel, "In the same New Bedford there stands a whalesman's chapel and few are the moody fishermen shortly bound for the Indian or Pacific Oceans who failed to make a Sunday visit to this spot." I guess all journeymen have similar thoughts.

Pick up Route 6 west by following signs to Interstate 195 west (the routes are parallel) and then follow Route 6 west to Route 177 west. Stay on Route 177 if you want to shorten the loop, or shoot down Route 88 for more beaches and more coast to explore. **Horseneck Beach** is a Massachusetts state park with day parking, camping, and a whole bunch of diverse people. Routes 179 and Route 77 are country two-laners bringing you to Tiverton, R.I. from Horseneck Beach. Pick up Route 24 south and enjoy the ride back home, following the shoreline.

Seamen's Bethel

The Inland Loop

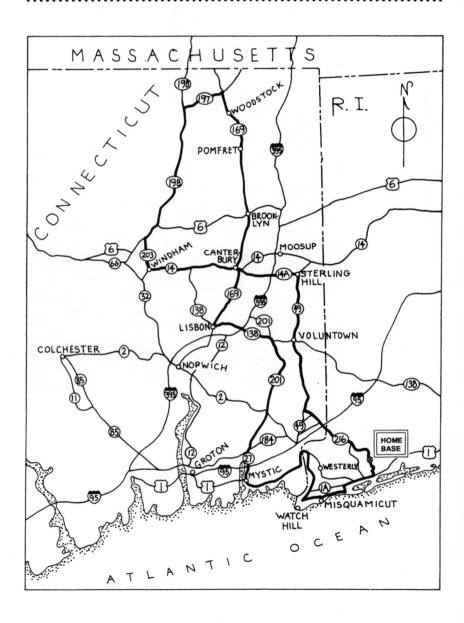

The Inland Loop

· ·

Distance   *175 miles (292 kilometers)*

Speed   *30 to 65* MPH *(50 to 108* KPH*)*

Highlights   *Scenic stretches, back roads, submarines, and ferris wheels*

The Route from Burlingame State Park

→ Right out of Burlingame State Park on to Cookestown Road to R.I. Route 216 north.

→ R.I. Route 216 north to Conn. Route 49 north just after Clarks Fall, Conn.

→ Route 49 north to Route 14A at Sterling Hill.

→ Route 14A west to Route 169 north at Canterbury.

→ Route 169 north to Route 197 west at N. Grosvenor.

→ Route 197 west to Rte 198 south at junction.

→ Route 198 south to Route 6 west at junction.

→ Route 6 west to Route 203 south at North Windham.

→ Route 203 south to Rte 14 east at Windham.

→ Route 14 east to Rte 169 south at Canterbury.

→ Route 169 south to Route 138 east at junction.

→ Route 138 east to Route 201 south at junction.

→ Route 201 south merges with Route 184 west just north of Old Mystic.

→ Route 184 west to Rte 27 south at Old Mystic.

→ Route 27 south to Route 1 east at Mystic.

→ Route 1 east to R.I. Route 1A east at Westerly, R.I.

→ Route 1A east to Watch Hill Road.

→ Round the point and follow coastal road east.

→ Take first public right to Atlantic Avenue and Misquamicut State Beach (there are signs), in Misquamicut.

→ Atlantic Avenue to Dunn's Corners Road at Weekapaug.

→ Dunn's Corners Road to Route 1A east at intersection.

→ Route 1A east to Route 1 east.

→ Route 1 east to Burlingame State Park.

Roseland, a Gothic among the Victorians, across from Woodstock Green

After all the tight quarters and museums of the Bay Loop, it's time to stretch our steeds a bit. The first 125 miles of this loop are scenic riding with some twists and room to wail (or should I say whale?). Take a right out of the campground onto Cookestown Road, a narrow two-lane twisty with some sand patches on the curves (reminds me of an old beach road) so don't open it up too much. Route 216 is like a country lane with pine tree stands; more throttle, please. Route 49 opens up even more, with forest on one side and rolling farmland on the other. Route 14A tightens with ascending and descending roads, another vote for east/west roads. Route 169 straightens and opens.

Many of the towns along this loop have statues to commemorate their American Revolution war heroes. In Brooklyn, Conn. stands the statue of General Israel Putnam, Esq. It was "Old Put" who, at the Battle of Bunker Hill, issued the command "Don't fire until you

Mystic Seaport

see the whites of their eyes!" Other towns honor their American Revolution heritage with historical plaques.

Route 197 west gets you going again with some tight curves. Route 198 is a remote road, so remote that as I was tooling along, I came across a fox just lying on the asphalt, warming in the sun.

Route 14 winds east to Route 169 and scenic farm-lands. Route 201 is a pretty country lane following the contours of the land.

OK, the exercise is over and it's back to civilization and history, i.e., **Mystic Seaport.**

This is the largest maritime museum in the United States. Located on 17 acres along the Mystic River, the museum is home to such ships as the Charles W. Morgan, the last wooden whaling bark of a fleet that numbered over 700 in the mid-1800s. A full working portrayal of sea and seaport life in the 1800s is here to explore: a ship chandlery, rigging loft, cooperage (cask and barrel making), sailor's tavern, and restoration

The strip, Misquamicut State Beach

shop, among other exhibits. Mystic Seaport is a popular place, so be prepared for the crowds. A visit can easily take a full day, depending on your fascination factor. Do not budget less than a half day to justify the $14 admission fee.

Back on the steed, grab Route 1 east into Rhode Island and head for **Watch Hill.** This village is a miniature Newport with huge mansions overlooking the sea. The town also boasts the world's oldest carousel, but it's for little kids only. Don't worry, though, **Misquamicut,** an original honky-tonk beach town, has all the big kid rides. Sporting ferris wheels, water slides, and N.Y.-style hot dogs (it's like a chili dog without the flame), Misquamicut has beach bars, deck bars, rock n'roll bars, discos, and general cruising at night. It's a fun place to be, and about 10 minutes from the campground. If you're imbibing, stay at one of the many motels on the strip.

Rejoin Route 1A at the end of the strip and follow it to Route 1 east to close the loop. If you are still hungry or thirsty, the **Four Seasons Restaurant** on the west/southbound side of Route 1, just before Burlingame State Park, has excellent food with some different approaches to familiar favorites: for example, Rhode

Island Clam Chowder. Unlike Manhattan chowder with a tomato base, or New England chowder with a milk base, Rhode Island chowder is in a clam juice broth with a touch of dill. The Four Seasons is usually crowded during the summer, so I ate at the bar and met some warm and friendly locals with tales ranging from building the USS Nautilus in Groton to collecting nautical artifacts for fun and profit.

Test drive old Hogs for a dollar.

The Above and Below Loop

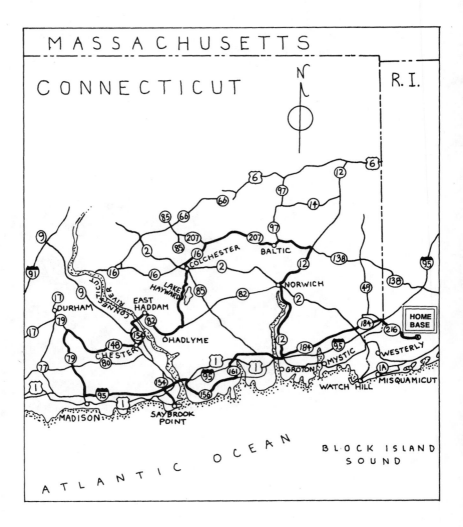

The Above and Below Loop

Distance *167 miles (278 kilometers)*

Speed *15 to 65* MPH *(25 to 108* KPH*)*

Highlights *Back roads, river roads, shoreline drives, some city traffic*

The Route from Burlingame State Park

→ Right, out of Burlingame State Park, onto Cookestown Road, to R.I. Route 216 north.

→ Conn. Route 216 north to Route 184 west just after passing Interstate 95.

→ Route 184 west to Route 12 north at Groton.

→ Route 12 north for 1.5 miles (USS NAUTILUS signs) to Crystal Lake Road. Return to Route 12 north.

→ Route 12 north to Route 138 west at Lisbon.

→ Route 138 west to Route 97 south at junction.

→ Route 97 south to Route 207 west at Baltic.

→ Route 207 west to Route 16 west at junction.

→ Route 16 west to Route 85 south at Colchester.

→ Route 85 south to Lake Hayward Road (first right after Route 2 underpass).

→ At fork, bear left onto Lake Shore Road.

→ At T, take right onto Haywardville Road.

→ Haywardville Road to Route 82 west (GILLETTE'S CASTLE signs) at intersection.

→ Route 82 west from Gillette's Castle.

→ Route 82 west to Route 154 south at Tylerville.

→ Route 154 south to Route 148 west at Chester.

→ Route 148 west to Route 79 south at junction.

→ Route 79 south to Route 1 north at Madison.

→ Route 1 north to Interstate 95 north at intersection.

→ Interstate 95 north to Route 156 south at exit after Connecticut River.

→ Route 156 south to Route 161 north at Niantic.

→ Route 161 north to Interstate 95 north at intersection.

→ Interstate 95 north to Route 184 east at Groton.

→ Route 184 east to Conn./R.I. Route 216 south at intersection.

→ R.I. Route 216 south to Cookestown Road to Burlingame State Park and home base.

Lighthouse Museum in Stonington

Shut the screen door, please.

Route 184 offers a country road alternative to both Interstate 95 and Route 1, a fact you can use for the previous loops. The **USS Nautilus and Submarine Museum** is definitely worth the visit. Outside the Museum are actual midget submarines used in early exploration during World War I and World War II by the German, Japanese, and Italian navies, respectively. As I entered the museum, an 11-foot model of Captain Nemo's Nautilus faced me (Where is my 30-foot bathtub when I need it?). The museum is geared for sound, sight, and touch. A recreated submarine attack center stirs the imagination when you hear the sounds of battle from "down below." You can also use real periscopes to see submarines head up the Thames to the sub pens in Groton, though I didn't see any on my visit.

The museum has two mini-theaters with five-minute continuous loop films. Upstairs is a 50-foot cutaway replica of the USS Gato and a film of actual World War II battle scenes, with U.S. subs attacking and sinking a fleet of Japanese surface ships. Then the incongruity hit me: the film is shown on a Hitachi television. Hmmmmm!

Now it's time for the real thing. Climbing aboard the USS Nautilus, SSN 571, standing on her deck, and

A prototype for the 1903 Harley???

preparing to go below, I anticipated coming face to face with what until now had been only a legend to me. The guards handed me a telephone-shaped device that provided a self-paced tour, and I descended into the world's first nuclear sub. Launched on January 21, 1954 by Mamie Eisenhower, the USS Nautilus was the first ship to cross the geographic North Pole, 90 degrees north! It is hard to believe that over a hundred men lived in such tight quarters. At the time, these were spacious. The museum is free. It is closed on Tuesdays.

Route 12 north meanders along the Thames River back to its headwaters, past Norwich, Conn., and Interstate 95, where you pick up Route 138. Routes 138, 97 and 207 are short scoots to get to Route 16. You can fly on Route 16 with soft bends and slow rollers till you reach Colchester. Route 85 merges in and out of town fast. Take the immediate right after you go under Route 2. It feels like you're going to grab the cloverleaf onto Route 2, but at the T bear left onto Lake Shore Road. This is a shady, lake-hugging, narrow road. The lake is inviting; the signs saying PRIVATE BEACH are not. I stopped at the third little beach, got a couple of stares from the more uptight folk, but no hassles. The water felt great, probably more so for being forbidden fruit.

The Devil's Hopyard State Park off of Hayward-ville Road offers a large park, campground, and a 60-foot waterfall.

The park is considered hallowed ground by the superstitious. The local folklore centers on the Devil's liking of wild and rugged scenery, embracing the park as his (or is that hers?). The other tale is of a traveler who, passing along the trail near a clearing where the hops were growing, saw mist-shrouded forms leaping from the ledges and trees in the hopyard. Zip that tent up tight!

From the superstitious we go to the superfluous, **Gillette's Castle** in Hadlyme. From Route 82 west, follow signs to the castle.

William Gillette, an actor, is credited with introducing Sherlock Holmes to American theater. He began construction of his castle in 1914 and finished in 1919.

Two hundred feet above the Connecticut River, with granite walls four to five feet thick and 24 rooms, Gillette's home reflects his eccentricity. He even built his own three-mile railroad to take guests down to the river.

Picking up Route 82 west brings you to the Connecticut River and the town of **East Haddam.** A small

Gillette's Castle

Goodspeed Opera House

town on the banks of the Connecticut River, it boasts the **Goodspeed Opera House,** a fully restored Victorian theater which offers films, musicals, and plays throughout the spring, summer, and fall.

The bridge next to the Goodspeed Opera House opens for passing ships by pivoting on its center support. Make sure the road matches up with the bridge before crossing the river, then head into the quaint village of Chester.

Chester is home to the **National Theater of the Deaf,** where plays are produced in sign language but are translated into words for hearing people, who make up 90 percent of the audience. The theater group travels internationally from September to March. If you are riding by in June, the theater group presents storytellings on Meetinghouse Green.

Route 148 west gets us back to our riding roots. The road is squiggly, has little traffic and is smooth. Route 79 south points us straight to the sea. Route 1 east/north, from Madison to Niantic, is a good place to do your road errands. This is a commercial strip with plenty of places to buy your supplies at low cost, high-volume stores. A couple of side roads off of Route 1 break up the commercial flow and bring you closer to

*Crossing the
Connecticut River
at Hadlyme*

the water. Route 154 dips quickly into Fenwick and Saybrook Point before rejoining Route 1 in Old Saybrook. Route 156 does the same type of dip as Route 154 just after the Connecticut River crossing. You can continue on Route 156 into New London, grab Interstate 95 north, drop down to Route 1 and retrace the previous Inland Loop.

Places of Interest

CONNECTICUT

Central Falls Devil's Hopyard, off Route 82. A remote place to camp or rest a weary traveler's bones!

Chester National Theater of the Deaf, 5 West Main Street. Phone (203) 526-4971 or (203) 526-4974 (TDD for hearing-impaired callers). Open May thru August, plus a Christmas Production. Call for schedule.

East Haddam Goodspeed Opera House, Route 82, 06423. Phone (203) 873-8668 for tickets; office (203) 873-8664. April through December. Office hours are 9:00 a.m. to 6:30 p.m. Performances as scheduled.

Groton USS Nautilus Memorial and Submarine Force Museum, Crystal Lake Road off Route 12. Phone (800) 343-0079. Open year-round; April 15 to October 15, 9:00 a.m. to 5:00 p.m.; 9:00 a.m. to 3:30 p.m. rest of the year. Closed Tuesdays. Free. Everything you wanted to know about submarines and their history.

Hadlyme Gillette Castle, 67 River Road, off Route 82. Phone (203) 526-2336. Open end of May to Christmas, 9:00 a.m. to 5:00 p.m. Expansive views of the Connecticut River and picnic spot. Admission $2.

Mystic Mystic Seaport, 50 Greenmanville Avenue (Route 27). Phone (203) 527-0711. Open year-round, July and August 9:00 a.m. to 8:00 p.m.; 9:00 a.m. to 5:00 p.m. rest of the year. A operational turn-of-the-century seaport and museum. Admission $14.

Stonington Old Light House Museum, 7 Water Street. Phone (203) 535-1440. Open May 1 to October 31, 10:00 a.m. to 5:00 p.m. Climb to the top of the lighthouse for a 360-degree view of Long Island Sound. Admission $2.

MASSACHUSETTS

Fall River Battleship Cove and Fall River Heritage State Park, Davol Street. Phone (800) 533-3194 and (508) 675-5759 respectively. Open year round. Times vary with seasons. Admission $6. AAA discount.

Marine Museum at Fall River, 70 Water Street. Phone (508) 674-3533. Open year round 10:00 a.m. to 4:30 p.m. If you're a Titanic or old steamship buff, this is your place. Admission $3.

New Bedford New Bedford Whaling Museum, 18 Johnny Cake. Phone (508) 997-0046. Open year-round 9:00 a.m. to 5:00 p.m. Monday through Saturday and 1:00 to 5:00 p.m. Sundays. Admission $3.50. AAA discount. Do It!

Seamen's Bethel, Johnny Cake Hill (across from the Whaling Museum). No phone. Open May to October. If you are here, then be there. A little bit of literary history. Read all the plaques of seamen lost! Donations accepted.

Westport Horseneck Beach State Reservation, Westport Point. Phone (508) 636-8816. Open mid-May to mid-October. Popular spot for both camping and beaching. Admission is $5 for the beach and $12 for a campsite.

RHODE ISLAND

Charlestown Burlingame State Park, U.S. Route 1. Phone (401) 322-7994. Excellent, spacious campground with 733 sites. Good spacing of sites. $10.00.

Jamestown Beavertail Lighthouse and State Park, Beavertail Road. Lighthouse is open June to August; park open year round. Beautiful views, spots to rest by the ocean's edge. Donations accepted.

Jamestown Harbor East Ferry Market & Deli, 47 Cononicus Avenue. Phone (401) 423-1592. Daily 6:30 a.m. to 5:00 p.m. Great coffee, pastries and location for reading the morning paper. $$

Misquamicut Misquamicut State Beach, Atlantic Avenue. This is an unattended open stretch of beach. Beach Blanket Bingo Bonanza meets Honky-Tonk City.

Newport Hammersmith Farm, Ocean Drive. Phone (401) 846-7346. Open April to mid-November. Last working farm in Newport. Admission $6.

Inn at Castle Hill, Ocean Drive. Phone (401) 849-3800. The views are unsurpassed from the backyard and patio. $$$

The Mansions, Bellevue Avenue. Information for any or all of the mansions can be obtained by calling (401) 847-1000. Open May to September daily. Varies by mansion at other times. Do one at least! Admission is $6 per mansion or $11 for any two.

Travel Information

CONNECTICUT

Connecticut Department of Economic Development, Tourism Division

865 Brook Street, Rocky Hill 06067. Phone (800) CT BOUND. Maps, brochures, campgrounds and state parks.

Southeastern Connecticut Tourism District

27 Masonic Street, P.O Box 89, New London 06320. Phone (800) 222-6783. Coastal information on lodging and attractions.

MASSACHUSETTS

Spirit of Massachusetts, Office of Tourism

100 Cambridge Street, Boston 02202. Phone (617) 727-3201. Guide by region, bed and bath directory, maps, and state parks, forests and campgrounds.

Bristol County Development Council

P.O. Box BR-976, New Bedford 02741. Phone (508) 997-1250. Southern coast of Massachusetts specifically and in detail.

RHODE ISLAND

Rhode Island Tourism Division

7 Jackson Way, Providence 02903. Phone (800) 556-2484. Ask for the visitor's guide and visitor's map. Both are excellent, with thorough guides to parks, beaches, attractions and local roads.

South County Tourism Council

P.O. Box 651, Narragansett 02882. Phone (800) 548-4662. Ask for the South County Beach Brochure and Tourism Booklet.

Emergency and Medical Assistance

CONNECTICUT

Groton Pequod Medical Center, Exit 88 off Interstate 95, Hazelnut Road. Phone (203) 446-8265.

New London Lawrence Memorial Hospital, 365 Montauk Avenue. Phone (203) 442-0711.

MASSACHUSETTS

Dartmouth Massachusetts State Police Barracks. Phone (508) 993-8373.

Fall River St. Anne's Hospital, 795 Middle Street. Phone (508) 674-5741.

New Bedford St. Luke's Hospital, 101 Page Street. Phone (508) 997-1515.

RHODE ISLAND

Newport Newport Hospital, Friendship Street. Phone (401) 846-6400.

North Kingstown State Police, Route 1, 7875 Post Road, Wickford Barracks. Phone (401) 294-3371.

Wakefield South County Hospital, 100 Kenyon Avenue. Phone (401) 782-8000.

Westerly The Westerly Hospital, Wells Street. Phone (401) 596-6000.

Appendix A – Finding Your Own Way

The fun begins with planning your journey. A road map contains vital information such as distances (and therefore time needed to complete a journey), road surfaces (which affect safety and comfort), and size of road (highway, byway, county, country). The key to making the road map a useful tool is the ability to glean this information from your map and apply it to the ride. I know of nothing more frustrating than stopping every ten minutes on a bumpy dirt road, in the dark, to reaffirm membership in the "Where-The-Hell-Are-We" club.

Most maps are oriented to north as the top border. This is true for state and regional maps as well as those in this book. Double-check, however, because specific city or small geography maps may pivot the north axis for easy reading. The right margin of the map (if the top is north) is east. That's the direction the sun will be rising in the morning.

The legend, which is similar to the index of a book, allows you to convert the map pictorial into useful information. An example is the mileage scale, which converts inches to miles or kilometers. This scale allows you to plan time and distance for the trip. The boldness (thickness) of the lines correspond to the size of the road. The boldest line represents interstate highways; the thinnest lines (my favorite) represent country back roads. The more squiggly the line, the more curvy the road!

Using the map as a navigation tool is easy if you apply a few simple techniques. First, study the map before you leave to determine the general direction to your destination. Take a look at the route and what physically is on the route, for example, mountains, rivers, lakes, grandma's house. What landmarks make for natural resting spots? How long to the first checkpoint (both time and mileage)?

Second, orient your map to your route. Since you can read a map from any direction, place the map in your tank bag with your destination at the top. For example, if you are taking a route to the east, place the easterly border of the map on top. Now you, the map, and the terrain are all aligned. It makes for easier landmark recognition. Fold the map so that only the panel representing the route is visible. The less time you spend looking down at the map, the more time you have your eyes on the road!

Hints

1. I find that a little research at the library can add a lot of richness and depth to my experience and memories of a ride. Libraries, whether in your home town or on the road, are accessible, free, hold a wealth of useful information, and are a great place to hide out from the wet stuff!

2. The information included with each journey identifies sources of good maps, but be sure to stop at any local real estate office for specific county maps. These maps will show even the smallest local roads, which are often the best for exploring.

3. As you are preparing for a trip, write down your route before you leave and place it in a corner of your map holder with one of those less-than-permanent sticky note pads, large enough to read yet small enough not to interfere with your map. List the route numbers in order. For example, the Northeast Notches loop di-

rections would be 16n-26e-2w-113s-16s. This will give you intersection references without making you orient yourself to the map at each interchange.

4.   An excellent guide to the sport of motorcycle touring, with help on selecting equipment, packing, dressing properly, handling emergencies, and general road smarts, is the book *Motorcycle Touring and Travel,* by Bill Stermer, available from Whitehorse Press, 154 West Brookline Street, Boston, MA 02118-1901.

Appendix B – Motorcycle Dealers

Following are dealers who sell and service the major brands in New England. While a list of this kind can never be completely accurate, it will nonetheless give you a shot at finding help on the road if you need it.

If you have a Suzuki, you can call their toll-free number to find the location of their other fine dealers. Call 1-800-255-2550.

DEALER (Alphabetical by state, then name of town)	BMW	Ducati	Harley-Davidson	Honda	Kawasaki	Moto Guzzi	Suzuki	Yamaha
Connecticut								
Berlin Motorcycle Sales 559 Wilbur Cross Hwy Berlin, CT 06037 Phone: (203) 828-6547				●				
Bill's Harley-Davidson 522 Boston Ave Bridgeport, CT 06610 Phone: (203) 334-6561			●					
Bridschges Kawasaki of Bristol 451 Broad St Bristol, CT 06010 Phone: (203) 583-0116					●			
Canton BMW, Inc. Rt 44 Canton, CT 06019-0591 Phone: (203) 693-6339	●					●		

DEALER (Alphabetical by state, then name of town)	BMW	Ducati	Harley-Davidson	Honda	Kawasaki	Moto Guzzi	Suzuki	Yamaha
Willows Kawasaki-Yamaha 1555 Highland Ave Cheshire, CT 06410 Phone: (203) 272-7201					●			●
Miller Specialties, Inc. 204-A East Main St Clinton, CT 06413 Phone: (203) 669-1926						●		
Michael Swider Motorcycles RFD 3 - West Rd Colchester, CT 06415 Phone: (203) 537-2297						●		
Burton L. Ives & Sons, Inc. 435 Rt 66 East Colombia, CT 06237 Phone: (203) 456-3274				●				
Danbury Cycle Ranch 37 Lake Avenue Extension Danbury, CT 06811 Phone: (203) 743-6508				●				
Marsh Motorcycle Co., Inc. 36 North Rd East Windsor, CT 06088 Phone: (203) 623-7795						●		
Frank DeGray Motorcycles Rt 83 Ellington, CT 06029-9755 Phone: (203) 872-2980	●							
T.S.I. Harley-Davidson Sales 390 Somers Rd Ellington, CT 06029 Phone: (203) 875-6663			●					
Enfield Motor Sports, Inc. 27 Palomba Dr Enfield, CT 06082 Phone: (203) 741-2173					●		●	●
N.E. Cycle Works, Inc. 661 Gold Star Hwy Groton, CT 06340 Phone: (203) 445-8158				●	●			

DEALER (Alphabetical by state, then name of town)	BMW	Ducati	Harley-Davidson	Honda	Kawasaki	Moto Guzzi	Suzuki	Yamaha
New London County Motorcycle Sales 1416 Gold Star Hwy Rt 184 Groton, CT 06340 Phone: (203) 445-9745			●					
Freedom Honda 2691 State St Hamden, CT 06517 Phone: (203) 288-8000				●				
Hartford Harley-Davidson Sales 249 Wawarme Ave Hartford, CT 06114 Phone: (203) 244-2213			●					
New England Cycle Center 73 Leibert Rd Hartford, CT 06120 Phone: (203) 527-0822								●
Manchester Honda 30 Adams St Manchester, CT 06040 Phone: (203) 646-2789				●				
Sullivan's Honda City 392 Washington St Middletown, CT 06457 Phone: (203) 347-3383				●				
Sippin Cycle Sales 234 Main St Monroe, CT 06468 Phone: (203) 261-3668				●				●
Lindner's Cycle Shop 21 Forest St New Caanan, CT 06840-4702 Phone: (203) 966-5188	●							
Brothers' Harley-Davidson, Inc. 347 Forbes Ave New Haven, CT 06512 Phone: (203) 468-1011			●					
Libby's Sales & Service, Inc. 60 Printers Lane New Haven, CT 06519 Phone: (203) 772-1112								●

DEALER (Alphabetical by state, then name of town)	BMW	Ducati	Harley-Davidson	Honda	Kawasaki	Moto Guzzi	Suzuki	Yamaha
New Haven Kawasaki 143 Whalley Ave New Haven, CT 06511 Phone: (203) 562-3900					•		•	
Honda/Kawasaki of New Milford 280 Danbury Rd, Rt 2 New Milford, CT 06776 Phone: (203) 355-3161				•	•			
Central Sports, Inc. 399 West Main St Norwich, CT 06360 Phone: (203) 886-2047				•	•			•
Adams Honda 808 Main St Oakville, CT 06779 Phone: (203) 274-6753				•				
Central Sports, Inc. Rt 12 Plainfield, CT 06374 Phone: (203) 564-3354				•				•
Kawasaki of Putnam, Inc. Upper School St, Rt 44 Putnam, CT 06260 Phone: (203) 928-7565					•			•
Midtown Kawasaki 1864 Silas Dean Hwy Rocky Hill, CT 06067 Phone: (203) 721-0193		•			•			
Harley-Davidson of Stamford 481 Canal St Stamford, CT 06902 Phone: (203) 975-1985			•					
Bill's Harley-Davidson 700 Lordship Blvd Stratford, CT 06497 Phone: (203) 380-2600			•			•		
D & J Harley-Davidson, Inc. 381 South Main St Thomaston, CT 06787 Phone: (203) 283-0251			•					

DEALER (Alphabetical by state, then name of town)	BMW	Ducati	Harley-Davidson	Honda	Kawasaki	Moto Guzzi	Suzuki	Yamaha
Cycle Performance, Inc. 923 Migeon Ave Torrington, CT 06790 Phone: (203) 489-6616					•		•	•
Family Cycle Center, Inc. 1223 North Main St Waterbury, CT 06704 Phone: (203) 757-7830				•				
Massachusetts								
Ronnie's Cycle Sales & Service 150 Howland Ave Adams, MA 01220 Phone: (413) 743-0715				•				•
Hogan's Cycle Shop 1782 Main St Agawam, MA 01001 Phone: (413) 786-9170		•						
Greater Boston Motorsports 1098 Massachusetts Ave Arlington, MA 02174-4313 Phone: (617) 648-1300	•			•	•			
Worcester County Honda/Yamaha 141 Washington St Auburn, MA 01501 Phone: (508) 757-9521				•				•
Aldo's Harley-Davidson, Inc. Rt 5 & 10 Bernardston, MA 01337 Phone: (413) 648-9302			•					
Cycles 128 107 Brimball Ave Beverly, MA 01915 Phone: (508) 927-3400				•				•
Eastern Cycle Salvage 87 Park St Beverly, MA 01915 Phone: (508) 922-3707		•						

DEALER (Alphabetical by state, then name of town)	BMW	Ducati	Harley-Davidson	Honda	Kawasaki	Moto Guzzi	Suzuki	Yamaha
Freeman Cycle 50 Federal St Beverly, MA 01915-5714 Phone: (508) 922-6668	•					•		
Billerica Yamaha Riveredge Rd off Rt 4 Billerica, MA 01862 Phone: (508) 459-4251								•
Brockton Cycle Center 2020 Main St Brockton, MA 02401 Phone: (508) 584-1451					•			•
Dunbar Motorcycles, Inc. 856 North Montello St, Rt 28 Brockton, MA 02401-1655 Phone: (508) 583-4380	•	•				•		
Lowell Honda Kawasaki 170 Tyngsboro Road North Chelmsford, MA 01863 Phone: (508) 251-4440				•	•		•	
Broderick's Cycle 385 Main St Dalton, MA 01226 Phone: (413) 684-3945		•						
Easthampton Harley-Davidson 2 Adams St Easthampton, MA 01027 Phone: (413) 527-1556			•					
Cycle Craft Co., Inc. 1813 Revere Beach Pkwy Everett, MA 02149 Phone: (617) 389-8888			•					
Parkway Cycle 1865 Revere Beach Pkwy Everett, MA 02149 Phone: (617) 389-6998					•		•	•
Gardner Cycles 204 East Broadway Gardner, MA 01440 Phone: (508) 632-6840						•		

DEALER (Alphabetical by state, then name of town)	BMW	Ducati	Harley-Davidson	Honda	Kawasaki	Moto Guzzi	Suzuki	Yamaha
A.J. Cycle Shop 147 C Rt 2 Gill, MA 01376-0147 Phone: (413) 863-9543	●							
Green River Honda/Kawasaki/Suzuki 52 River St Greenfield, MA 01301 Phone: (413) 774-2893				●	●		●	
Ray's Cycle Center, Inc. 332 Wells St Greenfield, MA 01301 Phone: (413) 773-8718								●
South Shore Kawasaki/Yamaha 972 Washington St Hanover, MA 02339 Phone: (617) 826-0771					●			●
Kawasaki/Yamaha/BMW of Cape Cod 405 West Main St Hyannis, MA 02601 Phone: (508) 775-6204	●				●			●
American Harley-Davidson 1437 Central St, Rt 12 Leominster, MA 01453 Phone: (508) 537-6919			●					
Ron's Cycle Sales 215 Lancaster St Leominster, MA 01453 Phone: (508) 537-6191						●		
Sky Cycle 402 Electric Ave Lunenburg, MA 01462 Phone: (508) 345-7360					●		●	●
Stanley Yamaha 201 W Grove St Middleboro, MA 02346 Phone: (508) 947-1217								●
Bernardi Cycles 671 Worcester Rd Natick, MA 01760 Phone: (508) 655-8586				●				

DEALER (Alphabetical by state, then name of town)	BMW	Ducati	Harley-Davidson	Honda	Kawasaki	Moto Guzzi	Suzuki	Yamaha
Archie's Scooter Service 489 Ashley Blvd New Bedford, MA 02745 Phone: (508) 995-9751				●				●
Morel's Cycle Shop 822 East Washington St North Attleboro, MA 02760 Phone: (508) 695-2061		●						
Harley-Davidson Freedom Center 220 Boston Rd North Billerica, MA 01862 Phone: (508) 663-6298			●					
Trailblazer Kawasaki/ North Reading Honda 49 Main St, Rt 28 North Reading, MA 01864 Phone: (508) 664-5461				●	●			
Valley Motorsports, Inc. 216 North King St Northampton, MA 01060 Phone: (413) 584-7303				●	●			
Al's Cycle Shop 165 Thorndike St Palmer, MA 01069 Phone: (413) 283-8233					●			
Cycle Design Rt 2A Phillipston, MA 01331 Phone: (508) 249-2244					●		●	
Bellstone Cycle, Inc. 1608 West Housatonic St Pittsfield, MA 01201 Phone: (413) 443-9407		●				●		
Berkshire Motor Works 180 South St Pittsfield, MA 01201 Phone: (413) 445-7775	●							
North Services, Inc. 675 Lenox Rd Pittsfield, MA 01201 Phone: (413) 499-3266				●				

DEALER (Alphabetical by state, then name of town)	BMW	Ducati	Harley-Davidson	Honda	Kawasaki	Moto Guzzi	Suzuki	Yamaha
Ronnie's Cycle Sales of Pittsfield 501 Wahconah St Pittsfield, MA 01201 Phone: (413) 443-0638			●		●			●
Harley-Davidson Cycle Center 730 MacArthur Blvd Pocasset, MA 02559 Phone: (508) 563-7387			●					
Pawtucket Motorcycle Sales 514 Winthrop St, Rt 44 Rehobeth, MA 02769 Phone: (508) 336-7516								●
G & G Cycles 226 Lafayette Rd Salisbury, MA 01952 Phone: (508) 462-7900		●			●			
Archie's M'cycle Sales & Srvc 19 Boston Turnpike Rd Shrewsbury, MA 01545 Phone: (508) 752-4856								●
Performance Cycles 939 Boston Turnpike, Rt 9 Shrewsbury, MA 01545 Phone: (508) 842-1068					●			
Riverside Motorcycle Sales 2 Union Square Somerville, MA 02143 Phone: (617) 628-6400		●			●			
Gifford Marine Co, Inc. 676 Dartmouth St South Dartmouth, MA 02748 Phone: (508) 996-8288				●				
Bob's Cycles Sales, Inc. 401 East Main St Southbridge, MA 01550 Phone: (508) 764-4643				●				
Baer's Cycle Sales, Inc. 11 Harvey St Springfield, MA 01119 Phone: (413) 783-2528					●			●

DEALER (Alphabetical by state, then name of town)	BMW	Ducati	Harley-Davidson	Honda	Kawasaki	Moto Guzzi	Suzuki	Yamaha
Tibby's Harley-Davidson Sales 227 Berkshire Ave Springfield, MA 01109 Phone: (413) 781-0785			●					
Kawasaki of Swansea 620 Grand Army Hwy, Rt 6 Swansea, MA 02777 Phone: (508) 672-2827					●			
Monty's Cycle Shop, Inc. 751 North Main St West Bridgewater, MA 02379 Phone: (508) 583-1172			●					
Bettencourt's Honda 31 South Main St West Bridgewater, MA 02379 Phone: (508) 587-1701		●		●				
Popoli's Honda/Yamaha Rt 20, Springfield Rd Westfield, MA 01085 Phone: (413) 562-5661				●				●
The Harley Store 1030 State Rd, Rt 6 Westport, MA 02790 Phone: (508) 674-5780			●					
Weymouth Honda 211 Main St Weymouth, MA 02188 Phone: (617) 337-7400				●				
N.F. Sheldon, Inc. 477 Southbridge St Worcester, MA 01610 Phone: (508) 757-0002			●					
Maine								
Augusta North Cntry H-D Sales North Belfast Ave Augusta, ME 04330 Phone: (207) 622-7994			●					
Central Maine Harley-Davidson R.R. 2, 7 Miles West Bangor, ME 04401-9612 Phone: (207) 848-5709			●					

DEALER (Alphabetical by state, then name of town)	BMW	Ducati	Harley-Davidson	Honda	Kawasaki	Moto Guzzi	Suzuki	Yamaha
Brunswick Cycle & Sled 145 Pleasant St Brunswick, ME 04011 Phone: (207) 729-3023		•				•		
Plourde's Harley-Davidson Laurette St Caribou, ME 04736 Phone: (207) 496-3211			•					
Sam's Sport & Ski Shop, Inc. 131 Main St Caribou, ME 04736 Phone: (207) 496-6912								•
Dexter Motor Sales 91 Church St Dexter, ME 04930 Phone: (207) 924-3259					•			•
Friend & Friend, Inc. 199 State St Ellsworth, ME 04605 Phone: (207) 667-4688				•	•			•
Street Cycles, Inc. 405 US Rt 1 Falmouth, ME 04105-1307 Phone: (207) 781-4763	•		•				•	
Roger's Sport Center 47 West Main St Fort Kent, ME 04743 Phone: (207) 834-5505								•
R & T Cycle Shop Highland Ave, Rt 3 Gardiner, ME 04345 Phone: (207) 582-6496				•				•
Reynold's Honda-Yamaha- Kawasaki RR 3, Box 257 Gorham, ME 04038 Phone: (207) 929-6641				•	•			•
Fred's Body Shop North Main St Greenville, ME 04441 Phone: (207) 695-3352								•

DEALER (Alphabetical by state, then name of town)	BMW	Ducati	Harley-Davidson	Honda	Kawasaki	Moto Guzzi	Suzuki	Yamaha
Peabody International 75 Bangor St Houlton, ME 04730 Phone: (207) 532-3573								•
Tidd's Sport Shop, Inc. Rt 2 Houlton, ME 04730 Phone: (207) 532-6476				•				
B & E Enterprises Rt 2 Jay, ME 04239 Phone: (207) 897-4211								•
Harley's-R-U.S. 839 Main St Lewiston, ME 04240 Phone: (207) 786-2822			•					
Schott Motorcycle Supply, Inc. Strawberry Ave Lewiston, ME 04240 Phone: (207) 784-1308				•				
Yvon's Track & Trail 1095 Main St Lewiston, ME 04240 Phone: (207) 782-5115		•						
Richards Sport Shop 339 West Broadway Lincoln, ME 04457 Phone: (207) 794-3363							•	•
Moose Horn Kawasaki Rt 4 North Jay, ME 04262 Phone: (207) 645-2057					•			
Maheu's, Inc. Rt 11 & 137 Oakland, ME 04963 Phone: (207) 465-2513					•			•
K.K. Motor Sports 645 Main St Presque Isle, ME 04769 Phone: (207) 764-7180				•	•			

DEALER (Alphabetical by state, then name of town)	BMW	Ducati	Harley-Davidson	Honda	Kawasaki	Moto Guzzi	Suzuki	Yamaha
Woodman's Cycles, Inc. 572 Main St Sanford, ME 04073 Phone: (207) 324-7500					●			●
Rod's Cycle Shop 37 Highland St Skowhegaw, ME 04976 Phone: (207) 474-6637		●						
Tri-Sports, Inc. 139 Main St, Rt 201 Topsham, ME 04086 Phone: (207) 729-3328				●	●			●
Rockport Kawasaki Rt 90 West Rockport, ME 04865 Phone: (207) 594-8134					●		●	●
Eagle's Sport Shop Rt 2, Box 647 Wilton, ME 04294 Phone: (207) 645-3733				●				
New Hampshire								
Sport Shack Honda Rt 16 South, Berlin-Gorham Line Berlin, NH 03570 Phone: (603) 752-2733				●				
Hood's Power East/ Hood's Suzuki RR 1, Box 269-H, Rt 11-103 Claremont, NH 03743 Phone: (603) 863-9900				●			●	●
Concord Motorcycle Shop, Inc. Basin & Sandquist St Concord, NH 03301 Phone: (603) 228-0364				●				
Freedom Suzuki-Yamaha of Concord 105 Manchester St Concord, NH 03301 Phone: (603) 225-2779							●	●

DEALER (Alphabetical by state, then name of town)	BMW	Ducati	Harley-Davidson	Honda	Kawasaki	Moto Guzzi	Suzuki	Yamaha
Heritage Harley-Davidson, Inc. 249 Loudon Rd Concord, NH 03301 Phone: (603) 224-3268			●					
Leighton's Kawasaki, Inc. RFD 2, Rt 125 (Lee) Dover, NH 03820 Phone: (603) 868-7550					●		●	●
Steve's Sport Center 20 Glen Rd Gorham, NH 03581 Phone: (603) 466-3921								●
Hamilton Sportcycles, Inc. 11 Hazel Dr Hampstead, NH 03841 Phone: (603) 329-7115		●						
Depot Honda 28 Depot Square Hampton, NH 03842 Phone: (603) 926-4581				●				
Hooksett Kawasaki 1354 Hooksett Rd Hooksett, NH 03106 Phone: (603) 668-4343					●			
Hudson Cycle Center Flagstone Dr Hudson, NH 03051 Phone: (603) 882-1573								●
Andy's Honda 48 Emerald St Keene, NH 03431 Phone: (603) 352-3555				●				
Monadnock Motorcycles 588 Monadnock Hwy Swanzey, NH 03446 Phone: (603) 352-1472			●					
Freedom Honda-Suzuki 533 State Rt 3 Laconia, NH 03246 Phone: (603) 524-6636				●				

DEALER (Alphabetical by state, then name of town)	BMW	Ducati	Harley-Davidson	Honda	Kawasaki	Moto Guzzi	Suzuki	Yamaha
Kawasaki-Yamaha of Laconia 1197 Union Ave Laconia, NH 03246 Phone: (603) 524-0100					•			•
Littleton Harley-Davidson, Inc. Rt 116 Littleton, NH 03561 Phone: (603) 444-1300			•					
White Mtn. Cycle & Marine RFD 2, Rt 135 Littleton, NH 03561 Phone: (603) 444-2944				•	•			
Cycle World, Inc. 168-170 Rockingham Rd Londonderry, NH 03053-2111 Phone: (603) 437-0290	•						•	
A-1 Sports Center 60 Beech St Manchester, NH 03101 Phone: (603) 668-1315								•
Manchester Harley-Davidson 20 Blaine St Manchester, NH 03102 Phone: (603) 622-2461			•					
Nault House of Wheels 150 John E Devine Dr Manchester, NH 03103 Phone: (603) 669-7220				•				
Meredith Harley-Davidson, Inc. Mill & Maple St Meredith, NH 03253 Phone: (603) 279-4526			•					
Second Wind BMW 4 Prospect St Milford, NH 03055 Phone: (603) 673-3120	•							
Amherst Motor Sports 535 Amherst St Nashua, NH 03063 Phone: (603) 889-2334						•		

DEALER (Alphabetical by state, then name of town)	BMW	Ducati	Harley-Davidson	Honda	Kawasaki	Moto Guzzi	Suzuki	Yamaha
Nashua Auto Company, Inc. 283 Main St Nashua, NH 03060 Phone: (603) 889-0161				●				
Kawasaki One Wheel Drive Box 3119, Main St North Conway, NH 03860 Phone: (603) 356-3522					●			
Adventure Suzuki, Inc. 34 Lafayette Rd North Hampton, NH 03862 Phone: (603) 964-8770								●
Seacoast Harley-Davidson, Inc. 90 Lafayette Rd, US Rt 1 North Hampton, NH 03862 Phone: (603) 964-9959			●					
Gilly's Cycle-Rama II, Inc. 107 Plaistow Rd Plaistow, NH 03865 Phone: (603) 382-4334								●
Dover Auto Supply 1850 Woodbury Ave Portsmouth, NH 03801 Phone: (603) 436-6200					●			
Dover Auto Supply, Inc. 445 High St Somersworth, NH 03878 Phone: (603) 742-9555				●				
New England Power Sports & Marine 13 Rockingham Rd Windham, NH 03087 Phone: (603) 893-0387				●				

DEALER (Alphabetical by state, then name of town)	BMW	Ducati	Harley-Davidson	Honda	Kawasaki	Moto Guzzi	Suzuki	Yamaha
New York								
Howard's Cycle Shop, Inc. Westside Dr Ballston Lake, NY 12019 Phone: (518) 399-4270								●
Bob's Lawn & Tractor Eqpt. Rt 22B Peru, NY 12972 Phone: (518) 643-8775					●			
North End Harley-Davidson 658 Cornelia St Plattsburgh, NY 12901 Phone: (518) 563-4360			●					●
Black Mt. Recreational Vehicles P.O. Box 45 Bolton Landing, NY 12814 Phone: (518) 745-0955								●
McDermott's Harley-Davidson Lake Sunnyside Rd Queensbury, NY 12804 Phone: (518) 792-2791			●					
Sportline Kawasaki Rt 9 Lake George Rd Queensbury, NY 12804 Phone: (518) 792-4655				●	●			

DEALER (Alphabetical by state, then name of town)	BMW	Ducati	Harley-Davidson	Honda	Kawasaki	Moto Guzzi	Suzuki	Yamaha
Rhode Island								
Honda/Yamaha Fun Center 1155 Tiogue Ave, Rt 3 Coventry, RI 02816 Phone: (401) 826-0600				●				
Kawasaki of Rhode Island 2706 S County Trail Rt 2 East Greenwich, RI 02818 Phone: (401) 884-2036					●			
Razee Auto & Motorcycle Ctr 730 Tower Hill Rd, Rt 1 North Kingston, RI 02852 Phone: (401) 295-8837	●	●		●		●		●
Dynamic Motors Kawasaki 210 West Ave Pawtucket, RI 02860 Phone: (401) 727-0510					●		●	
Precision Harley-Davidson, Inc. 269 Armistice Blvd Pawtucket, RI 02860 Phone: (401) 724-0100			●					
Berdic Kawasaki 15 Wm. South Canning Blvd Tiverton, RI 02878 Phone: (401) 624-6656					●		●	
Ocean State Harley-Davidson 60 Alhambra Rd Warwick, RI 02886 Phone: (401) 732-3646			●					

DEALER (Alphabetical by state, then name of town)	BMW	Ducati	Harley-Davidson	Honda	Kawasaki	Moto Guzzi	Suzuki	Yamaha
Vermont								
Harry J. Wilkins Upper Farwell St Barre, VT 05641 Phone: (802) 476-6104			●					
Dirt Works Cycle 2312 West Rd, Rt 9 Bennington, VT 05201 Phone: (802) 447-8606		●						
Burlington Harley-Davidson 696 Pine St Burlington, VT 05401 Phone: (802) 864-7464			●					
Central Vermont Kawasaki Rt 4A Center Rutland, VT 05736 Phone: (802) 438-2253					●			
Frank's M'cycle Sales and Svc Rt 15 Essex Center, VT 05451-0282 Phone: (802) 878-3930	●							
Land Air 46 Kellog Rd Essex Junction, VT 05452 Phone: (802) 878-5052				●				
Bevins' Marine & Cycle Center 407 Barre St Montpelier, VT 05602 Phone: (802) 223-2346					●			
Honda Unlimited 184 River St Montpelier, VT 05602 Phone: (802) 223-5651								●
Just Imports 79 Barre St Montpelier, VT 05602 Phone: (802) 229-5754	●						●	
Dan Turco and Sons Rt 7 North Clarendon, VT 05759 Phone: (802) 773-8650								●

DEALER (Alphabetical by state, then name of town)	BMW	Ducati	Harley-Davidson	Honda	Kawasaki	Moto Guzzi	Suzuki	Yamaha
Senesac Yamaha, Inc. RD 2, Box 175 St. Albans, VT 05478 Phone: (802) 527-1785								●
A.J.'s Honda-Kawasaki RFD 1, Rt 105 St. Albans, VT 05478 Phone: (802) 524-6565				●	●			
Greenwood Sales & Service Rt 5 - Memorial Dr St. Johnsbury, VT 05819 Phone: (802) 748-2730								●
Cyclespeed Rt 100 Waitsfield, VT 05673 Phone: (802) 496-6001		●						
North Country Power Sport Rt 30 Wells, VT 05774 Phone: (802) 645-0873				●				
Roadside Marine, Inc. Rt 2, Industrial Ave Williston, VT 05495 Phone: (802) 863-5523					●			●

Index

Index

Index

Other Popular Books For Adventurers

Motorcycle Journeys Through the Alps
by John Hermann

A journey through the Alps is an adventure not to be missed. With this comprehensive guidebook you can be certain you won't overlook any of the roads, mountain passes, or valleys that make this the one of the most alluring motorcycling regions in the world. The book contains detailed route descriptions and plenty of useful advice to help you avoid hassles and inconvenience, so that not a precious moment of your vacation is wasted.

You'll be prepared for situations the average Alps traveler might never anticipate, such as how to deal with automated European gas stations, and how to decipher European road signs. You'll know which hotels are hidden treasures and which ones to avoid. You'll even learn where the police like to hide to nab overzealous motorcyclists.

All of the region's important roads and passes are described and critiqued with Hermann's star system (two stars means a "must-ride" road). The book describes over 50 individual trips, each lasting about a day, giving you plenty of material for months of riding. From the Grossglockner, to the Dolomites, to the Lauterbrunnen Valley, to King Ludwig's Palace, every important road, pass, and scenic landmark is described with fascinating attention to detail. You'll find information on shops and restaurants, villages, and little-known spots where the views are unbelievably spectacular.

Hermann's informed, witty descriptions are dotted with local customs, history, and amusing travel anecdotes that are sure to enrich your journey. Read this book before your trip (and be sure to pack it with you) and you'll begin to appreciate what makes the Alps a motorcycling paradise.

John Hermann has over 20 years of riding experience and, as he was writing this book, completed his 26th motorcycle trip in the Alps. He is an acknowledged authority on Alps touring, having travelled alone and with tour groups. His wisdom and experience make this book an essential resource for anyone planning — or even considering — an Alpine adventure.

Paper, 5-1/2 x 8-1/2 inches, 223 pages, 126 illustrations. **HERM $19.95**

Motorcycle Journeys Through Baja
by Clement Salvadori

Join Clement Salvadori, one of the most popular motorcycle journalists of our day, as he personally leads you on a tour South of the Border. From TJ to Cabo, Salvadori knows Baja, having been a regular explorer of this grand peninsula for more than twenty years. Somewhere in between the must-see and the better-left-to-your-imagination spots of tourism and commerce, exists nearly 800 miles of the real thing: luxuriously uninhabited beaches, charming adobe missions, quaint fishing villages—most as yet unspoiled by modern man.

Unlike other guidebooks, *Motorcycle Journeys Through Baja* rates road conditions from the saddle of a bike, being frank in its evaluations of both the rugged and the tame. Accommodations get the same entertaining, honest treatment as the roads! But, did we mention the food? No worries, Salvadori does, and with the enthusiasm of a cafe gourmand. With an irreverent and enlightening commentary, the author ticks off resources and attractions, milepost by milepost, logging the quirky details that make traveling with him a delightful discovery. And no question about it, all your questions will be answered regarding necessary paperwork, legal considerations, insurance, personal health, useful phrases of Spanish (". . . Mi moto es muy rapido . . ."), road sign translations, and additional sources of information.

You've probably enjoyed Salvdori's taste for the open road (both paved and unpaved) in his many articles as a senior editor for both *Rider* and *American Rider* magazines. The next best thing to traveling with Clement Salvadori, is following his tracks as they disappear over the southern horizon. This book will point the way.

Paper, 5-1/2 x 8-1/2 inches, 240 pages, 125 illustrations. **SALV $19.95**

Other Popular Books For Adventurers

Motorcycle Journeys Through the Southwest
by Marty Berke

Marty Berke is back with his latest guide to America's scenic backroads and byways. This time, Marty's wanderlust has taken him to the American Southwest, where mountains, desert, roads, and sunny weather combine for ideal riding.

With this book you'll discover the best touring roads the Southwest has to offer. Arizona, New Mexico, Colorado, and Utah are all thoroughly detailed in this entertaining and informative guide.

The book describes 66 separate rides, each about a day in length. Each trip has been designed to include both great roads and great scenery, capturing all the grandeur and natural beauty of the region and introducing you to places and sights you might never find on your own. Visit Ouray, Colorado, home of the Wiesbaden Hot Springs and Vapor Caves; or the Chiricahua National Monument, where spires and columns of precariously balancing rocks seem to defy gravity. The Southwest is brimming with unique and colorful places, many of them little-known gems that are refreshingly free of tourist mobs.

Berke has scouted out the region's best campgrounds, parks, scenic landmarks, and restaurants, always keeping a sharp eye for the best bargains, to help you get the most out of your travel dollar. Each chapter contains useful listings of all points of interest, with information on prices, hours of operation, and other helpful tips.

Reviewers have had high praise for this popular addition to the Whitehorse Press Touring Guide series:

"**If you're going to the Durango rally, or just want to go riding in the west, this book is a must.**" . . . — *BMW Owners News*

"**Berke is a full-time motorcycle explorer and author, with an obvious sense of both curiosity and humor that makes this book as fun to read as it is useful.**" — *Motorcycle Consumer News*

"**If you have a taste for the offbeat, and want to avoid traditional tourist traps while experiencing the Southwest's finest motorcycling roads, then *Motorcycle Journeys through the Southwest* is for you.**" — *Keystone Motorcycle Press*

Paper, 5-1/2 x 8-1/2 inches, 430 pages, 150 illus.   **MJSW $24.95**

Motorcycle Journeys Through the Appalachians
by Dale Coyner

Amish farmers, bluegrass music, Elvis memorabilia, reminders of the War Between The States—the roots of America grow deep in the Appalachians. With *Motorcycle Journeys Through the Appalachians* by Dale Coyner, you can explore the scenic mountain vistas and bucolic valleys of a part of the country that's historically rich, culturally diverse, and laced with enticing roads.

This book lays out 35 day-long routes through Pennsylvania, Maryland, Virginia, West Virginia, and the Carolinas, all the while offering local lore, useful advice, and easy-to-follow directions from an author who can trace his Appalachian roots back several generations. Coyner's affection for his native region is obvious in every chapter: his lyrical descriptions of the best roads lead to lovingly detailed depictions of ancient caverns, covered bridges, rolling farm country, Civil War battlefields, and presidents' homes. Whether you're looking for living history or simply trying to find a glass-smooth, perfectly banked road, Coyner will point the way. You'll visit the cottage of Confederate spy Belle Boyd; get lost on scenic Virginia Route 231; pay homage to the Harley-Davidson Motor Company at its factory in York, Pennsylvania; loop through the mountain passes of the Blue Ridge Parkway; and find out why you shouldn't take anything about West Virginia for granted. You'll also chuckle at Coyner's descriptions of good ol' boys and marvel at his nuggets of historical lore. Detailed maps make navigation a breeze, while an appendix of local motorcycle dealers is insurance against a breakdown. Along the way, Coyner also points out the region's most rider-friendly restaurants, hotels, and campgrounds, ranging from bare-bones accommodations to spoil-yourself luxury.

Paper, 5-1/2 x 8-1/2 inches, 319 pages, 108 illus.   **COYN $19.95**

ORDER FORM FOR BOOKS

· ·

Whitehorse Press
P.O. Box 60
North Conway, NH 03860 - USA   *(UPS will not deliver to a P.O. box)*

SOLD TO: **UPS SHIPPING ADDRESS:** *(If different):*

Name: _____   Name: _____

Street: _____   Street: _____

City: _____   City: _____

State: _____ Zip: _____   State: _____ Zip: _____

Daytime Phone: (_____) _____   *(Speeds orders if we have a question.)*

How Many	Item Code	Description	Price Each	Total Price Dollars	Cents
		Prices subject to change without notice.	Subtotal		
			Shipping & Handling		
			Total Payment		

Order Toll-Free: 800-531-1133
(603-356-6556 Worldwide)
Order by FAX: 603-356-6590

SHIPPING and HANDLING:

U.S.: Add 10% of the total order; not less than $4.00.
On request, we will ship by overnight delivery;
call us for shipping rates.
Canada and Mexico:
Add 20% of the total order; not less than $5.00 U.S.

Other Countries:
We ship by air mail and charge actual cost.
Estimate $10.00 for first book, and $8.00 for each
additional book, or you may call for a quote.

PAYMENT: *(payment required before shipment)*

Credit card: ( ) Master Card   ( ) VISA   ( ) Amex   ( ) Check   ( ) Money Order   (U.S. dollars only)

.__.__.__.__.__.__.__.__.__.__.__.__.__.__.__.__.   Expiration Date _____ / _____
Credit Card Number *(please show spaces used in number)*

Name on Card: _____   Signature: _____

Thanks for your order!   **BERKins98**

About the Author

....

Marty Berke wrote *Motorcycle Journeys Through New England* out of a lifelong love of the open road. The resident of Wayland, Mass., caught the two-wheeled touring bug with his first Schwinn, and graduated to the motorized species not long afterward with a 1955 Vespa, a driver's license, and a $50 IOU to Mom.

After graduating from C.W. Post College with a degree in economics, Marty joined the international division of a large high-tech corporation and spent fifteen years pursuing his hobby—touring—while setting up new businesses and marketing programs throughout Europe, the Americas, the South Pacific, and Asia.

Marty now focuses on finding good roads and new ways to share them with you. His latest book is *Motorcycle Journeys Through the Southwest U.S.*, coming in the summer of 1994 from Whitehorse Press.